Benjamin Williams
LEADER RA
1831–1923

His Life and Paintings

The Skirts of a Pine Wood. Signed and dated 1896. 72 x 48in (183 x 122cm).   Photograph: Courtesy of Sotheby's, N.Y.

Benjamin Williams
LEADER RA

1831–1923

His Life and Paintings

RUTH WOOD MA

ANTIQUE COLLECTORS' CLUB

Dedicated
to
Christopher John Wood
(friend and ex-husband)
whose sponsorship made this book possible

British Library Cataloguing-in-Publication Data
A catalogue record for this book is available from the British Library

Published and printed in England by the Antique Collectors' Club Ltd.,
Woodbridge, Suffolk on Consort Royal Era Satin from
Donside Mill, Aberdeen, Scotland

The Antique Collectors' Club

The Antique Collectors' Club was formed in 1966 and quickly grew to a five figure membership spread throughout the world. It publishes the only independently run monthly antiques magazine, *Antique Collecting*, which caters for those collectors who are interested in widening their knowledge of antiques, both by greater awareness of quality and by discussion of the factors which influence the price that is likely to be asked. The Antique Collectors' Club pioneered the provision of information on prices for collectors and the magazine still leads in the provision of detailed articles on a variety of subjects.

It was in response to the enormous demand for information on 'what to pay' that the price guide series was introduced in 1968 with the first edition of *The Price Guide to Antique Furniture* (completely revised 1978 and 1989), a book which broke new ground by illustrating the more common types of antique furniture, the sort that collectors could buy in shops and at auctions rather than the rare museum pieces which had previously been used (and still to a large extent are used) to make up the limited amount of illustrations in books published by commercial publishers. Many other price guides have followed, all copiously illustrated, and greatly appreciated by collectors for the valuable information they contain, quite apart from prices. The Price Guide Series heralded the publication of many standard works of reference on art and antiques. *The Dictionary of British Art* (now in six volumes), *The Pictorial Dictionary of British 19th Century Furniture Design, Oak Furniture* and *Early English Clocks* were followed by many deeply researched reference works such as *The Directory of Gold and Silversmiths,* providing new information. Many of these books are now accepted as the standard work of reference on their subject.

The Antique Collectors' Club has widened its list to include books on gardens and architecture. All the Club's publications are available through bookshops world-wide and a full catalogue of all these titles is available free of charge from the addresses below.

Club membership, open to all collectors, costs little. Members receive free of charge *Antique Collecting*, the Club's magazine (published ten times a year), which contains well-illustrated articles dealing with the practical aspects of collecting not normally dealt with by magazines. Prices, features of value, investment potential, fakes and forgeries are all given prominence in the magazine.

Among other facilities available to members are private buying and selling facilities and the opportunity to meet other collectors at their local antique collectors' clubs. There are over eighty in Britain and more than a dozen overseas. Members may also buy the Club's publications at special pre-publication prices.

As its motto implies, the Club is an organisation designed to help collectors get the most out of their hobby: it is informal and friendly and gives enormous enjoyment to all concerned.

For Collectors — By Collectors — About Collecting

ANTIQUE COLLECTORS' CLUB
5 Church Street, Woodbridge, Suffolk IP12 1DS, UK
Tel: 01394 385501 Fax: 01394 384434
——————— or ———————
Market Street Industrial Park, Wappingers' Falls, NY 12590, USA
Tel: 914 297 0003 Fax: 914 297 0068

Acknowledgements

To name all those who have assisted me, regardless of how little, in the research and writing of this book would require a book on its own. Even though I shall mention a few names, it does not mean I have forgotten the many. My deepest thanks extend to you all.

My first thanks and undying gratitude must go to Tony Jerram for his unwavering patience in reading the drafts as I wrote them, correcting my endless grammatical mistakes and sending me on the trail for relevant information. He was my 'lifeline' when I was floundering around in a sea of unclarified ideas.

My sincere thanks to the artist's granddaughters, Mrs J. Clementi-Smith, Mrs P. Critchly, Mrs P. Stagg and Mrs A. Stead and her daughter Mrs R. Dick-Eland for allowing me to look through, and use, family documents and photographs. Also the personal reminiscences of their grandfather have allowed me to gain an insight into the man behind the paintings.

Thank you to all the art dealers who have very kindly allowed me either to go through their stock books or submitted lists of Leader paintings which have passed through their galleries. I am also grateful for their photographs of Leader's paintings and permission for reproduction either in the book and/or catalogue. A special thanks to the directors of Frost & Reed, Tony Neville and Charles Kingsett, who permitted me to copy the artist's Diaries, Sales Records of Paintings Sold and Account Books which are held at their gallery.

My thanks to all those at the auction houses, especially at Christie's, Sotheby's, Phillips and Bonhams, for the enormous help given and permission, not only to search through their catalogues and photographic library, but also permission to reproduce their photographs in both book and catalogue.

Special thanks to Martin Beisly and Jane Hollond, Christie's Victorian Pictures, for their continual encouragement for this book. Also to Veronique Gunner, Sotheby's Victorian Pictures.

My thanks to all the curators and trustees of public museums and art galleries throughout Britain and abroad for information about B.W. Leader paintings in their collections and permission to use their illustrations. Special thanks to Deborah Dean, Curator of paintings at the Worcester City Museum and Art Gallery for all her support in my promotion of Leader in the city where he was born.

My thanks also to all the staff who have assisted me in the many libraries and record offices that I have either worked in or contacted requesting information. To the private owners who have courteously allowed me into their homes to see and photograph their Leader paintings and generously given permission for reproduction – thank you.

To Peter Bradly and Robert Cotton, for their expertise as professional photographers, in producing a number of high quality reproductions required for the book – my thanks.

To Terry Parker, author of *Golden Hours: The Paintings of Arthur J. Elsley, 1861-1952,* and *The Guide to Pears' Prints,* for his enormous help in locating articles on the artist and giving me valuable leads.

I cannot forget to mention my friends whose patience and understanding was much appreciated in my need for solitude and concentration when writing. Special thanks are extended to those kind neighbours who have uncomplainingly looked after my home and pets when I have been away researching and to those tolerant friends, especially Diana and Martin Barnes, who have given me a bed and meals while on such trips.

Penultimately, my sincere thanks are extended to two people with the same name, Christopher Wood. One, a respected author on Victorian paintings, for reading and approving the final manuscript. The other Christopher, my ex-husband, without whose continued friendship and sponsorship this book would never have found a publisher.

Finally I must thank Diana Steel of the Antique Collectors' Club for bringing this book to completion so that Benjamin Williams Leader RA may not be forgotten.

Ruth Wood, MA 1998.

The Babbling Brook.
Signed and dated 1880.
36 x 60in. (91.5 x 152.5cm).
Photograph: Courtesy
Richard Green

Contents

		Page
Acknowledgements		6
Introduction		8
Background and Formative Years		10
Bid for Fame Part 1: 1857 – 1862		22
Bid for Fame Part 2: 1863 – 1870		35
Bid for Fame Part 3: 1871 – 1882		46
Recognition and Success Part 1 : 1883 – 1888		66
Recognition and Success Part 2 : 1889 – 1898		77
Sunset Years 1899–1923		91
End–Notes		112
Appendix 1:	'Pall Mall Gazette', 4.5.1886, p.11	121
Appendix 2:	'Pall Mall Gazette', 16.8.1886, p.2	122
Appendix 3:	Selective list of private collectors of B.W. Leader's paintings during the artist's lifetime.	123
Appendix 4:	List of B.W. Leader's painting's exhibited at the Royal Academy, 1854 -1923	128
Appendix 5:	Prints, known to be commercially produced from B.W. Leader's paintings and paintings reproduced for magazines and journals which were acknowledged with the words 'with permission of the owner of the copyright of the large plate'	132
Bibliography		139
Index		142

Introduction

For Shakespeare's Juliet a name was of no importance,[1] but for Benjamin Williams Leader RA, 1831-1923, it did matter a great deal. It assisted the advancement of his artistic career with the result that he became, during his lifetime, one of the most widely acclaimed Victorian landscape painters.

Today, although his paintings are held in many public and private collections in Britain and abroad and command high prices when they appear on the art market, the tendency is to discuss Leader in rather vague generalized terms within the context of Victorian landscape painting. Little is known about the artist himself, or why he painted what he did in a style uniquely his own.[2] For this reason the author believes a long overdue reassessment of Leader is necessary, the only other definitive work on the artist being an article written by Lewis Lusk in *The Art Annual* in 1901.[3] (Leader's career continued for another twenty years).

The main objective of this book is to place Leader and his paintings in the context of his age, a task which has not been without difficulty because of his long life which spanned three generations. His career extended from the early 1850s to 1923, twenty-two years beyond Queen Victoria's reign. An additional problem has been the stylistic evolution in British landscape painting over this period, an evolution which has to take into account the advent of photography and its taking over the functional role of reproducing exactly what is seen. It led artists to produce landscapes which, while still being faithful representations of nature, had to be imbued with that special artistic insight into nature to merit their works as art.

When Leader embarked on his career in the 1850s there was a flowering of the 'British School' of landscape painting. He was not, as would be expected, influenced by the established popular English exponents of landscape of the time, such as Thomas Creswick RA (1811-1869), and Frederick R. Lee RA (1798-1879), but was content, as many aspiring young artists were, to follow the Pre-Raphaelite artists' tenets to copy nature faithfully. A modification of the Pre-Raphaelites' detailed and time-consuming style had by the 1860s led to a more naturalistic portrayal of nature and Leader was seen by the art critics of the day as one of the representatives of the 'New Naturalistic British School' of landscape painting. Whilst his work from this period owes much to his study (and admiration) of the landscapes by John Constable (1776-1837), John Linnell (1792-1882), and the French Barbizon School, Leader acquired the confidence and facility to develop an independent style.

By 1880 he had become a master at exploiting differing natural effects of light, especially the amber luminosity from the late afternoon sun, which became his trade mark. He also produced freer, almost impressionistic, landscapes. These were mainly cabinet pictures and *plein-air* oil sketches and studies, preparatory work for the larger, more finished pictures he exhibited at the Royal Academy Summer Exhibitions. Leader exhibited two hundred and sixteen paintings at the Royal Academy over sixty-nine years from 1854, including the three small oil sketches exhibited posthumously in 1923 (see Appendix 4). These Academy paintings comprised only about eight per cent of his total output which perhaps is not surprising when one considers he was painting for much of his career for a new, prosperous class of the Victorian public who were insatiable collectors of art.

The Industrial Revolution was an era of opportunity, enterprise, and nationalism when anything 'British' was believed to be best. It was an era which greatly benefited the British artist whose patrons were the entrepreneurs - the merchants, manufacturers, brewers and bankers, many of whom had accumulated large fortunes - because there was now an economic base on which British Art was able to thrive (see Appendix 3 for a selected sample of patrons who accquired paintings by Leader). It was also an age which saw the emergence of both the professional art dealer and the art critic, both acting as intermediaries between the artist and the public. They were the real dictators of taste on whom the artist depended to advance his reputation and financial success. The prolific growth of the printed media, especially the art journals and magazines, could also enhance the reputation of the artist, bringing his work to the attention of a wider audience. For the first time, the non-exhibition-going public had access to an artist's work by means of the art magazines publishing engravings of his paintings. Superior quality reproductions were also offered for sale by the art dealers wishing to promote, and to sustain the popularity of, specific artists whose original paintings adorned their gallery walls (see Appendix 5 for engravings/etchings made after paintings by Leader).

I have chosen to divide this book into four main parts addressing the most important phases in the life and artistic career of Leader, beginning with his family background and formative years in Worcestershire, a county from which arose three other notable contemporaries: the composer and musician Sir Edward Elgar (1857-1934), the sculptor Sir Thomas Brock RA (1847-1922) and the novelist Mrs Henry Wood (1814-1887). The subsequent parts cover Leader's developing years, when he was seriously promoting himself as a professional artist in his bid for fame, his recognition and financial success, and the final 'sunset' years which were spent in the county of Surrey.

The one major source, not hitherto utilized, which inspired me to continue researching the artist, initially for my Master's Dissertation and now this book, were the artist's Diaries.[4] They cover an important period from 1857, when he changed his name, to 1898, the year he became a full member of the Royal Academy. The Diaries, often left blank for days and sometimes months are mainly a record of his artistic career and work practice. They reveal a serious-minded man, preoccupied with his status as a professional artist, obsessed with achieving recognition at the most important art institution, the Royal Academy. We learn nothing of Leader's social and political views and gain only glimpses of his acquaintances and family life. Because of the limited period covered by the Diaries, and the need to substantiate their content, extensive research into contemporary sources has been necessary. These sources include art critics' reviews of exhibitions printed in newspapers and journals, catalogues, letters and archive material together with current material, including that owned by the artist's direct descendants, together with personal recollections of the artist himself.

Where I have directly quoted from the Diaries, grammatical changes have been made for easier reading because Leader had the habit of writing in shorthand.

Portrait of Sarah Williams. Oval miniature. Board.
Private Collection. Photograph: R.Cotton.

Background and Formative Years

Benjamin Williams Leader's family name was Williams. Born on 12 March, 1831 in Worcester, he was the third of eleven children, second son, of Sarah and Edward Leader Williams. His birth date and the name Benjamin Williams were entered into the Quaker Birth Register at the Worcester Monthly Meeting of the Religious Society of Friends.[1] Against the entry were the letters 'NM', which meant that one or both parents were non-members, 'disowned'. It is believed that whilst Sarah (neé Whiting), born 1801 in Reading in the county of Berkshire to an umbrella maker, was a Quaker by birthright,[2] Edward, also born in same town in 1802[3] to an ironmonger, was a non-Friend (there is a memorial to his parents at Kings Road Baptist Church, Reading). To support this view, the couple had perforce to be married in 1827 at the parish church of Saint Giles, Reading. The consequence of such a marriage before a priest was 'disownment'.[4] The marriage certificate stated that Edward Leader Williams was already living in Worcester, although it is not known for what reason or in what year he took up residence there. The earliest reference to Benjamin's parents in Worcester was 1828, the same year as the birth of their eldest son Edward Leader Williams who was named after his father. In the Quaker Birth Register it stated that the place of birth was the High Street, in the Parish of Saint Helens, Worcester.[5] This was the birth place of the first four children[6] and as Mr. Williams' profession was an ironmonger,[7] following his father's trade, with premises at 94 High Street,[8] one can only assume that Benjamin was born in the family quarters 'above' the shop. This being true it certainly would have been conveniently forgotten in later life by one who had climbed the social ladder and become a respected and successful Royal Academician.

Benjamin's first experience of painting seems to have been due to his exposure, from childhood, to the artistic life of Worcester where his father had taken a leading role in the promotion of modern British Art in that rather conservative cathedral town. In April 1834, when Benjamin was three, his father, as Honorary Secretary of the Worcester Scientific and Literary Institute, announced that an important exhibition of modern British artists would be held in June at the Institute's new building, the 'Athenaeum'.[9] The underlying motives behind such an exhibition combined patriotic and business acumen on both a local and national level. The exhibition was also, no doubt, conceived in a spirit of 'friendly' rivalry with other large

Portrait of Edward Leader Williams. Oval miniature. Board.
Private Collection. Photograph: R.Cotton.

industrial cities, such as Birmingham, whose exhibitions of modern British Art were popular and returning increasing dividends. The 'Address' prefixed to the exhibition catalogue, which Mr Williams most probably helped to draft, stated that such societies had:

> . . . not been founded for show and indulgence of taste
> alone, but from an absolute necessity of using the best
> efforts of the UK to serve our Manufacturing and
> Commercial superiority against all foreign rivalry . . .They
> were intended to operate by their example, so as to create
> a national spirit of exertion for the encouragement of the
> Fine Arts.[10]

An earlier report, in 1816, by a Select Committee of the House of Lords on the Elgin Marbles, also inspired the Worcester-based authors of the Address to draw a comparison between the spirit of Athens at its highest epoch of culture and prosperity with its 30,000 free citizens, and Worcester with its 25,000.[11] Whilst similar exhibitions had already been held in Worcester by the local Society of Arts these seemed to be confined to paintings by artists residing in the area. For the 1834 exhibition invitations, probably in the form of a circular letter, were extended to members of the Royal Academy to submit their works. Artists, including the Royal Academicians William Etty, H.W. Pickergill, James Ward, John Constable, Howard Jones (the Professor of Painting), Alfred E. and John J. Chalon took advantage of such a venue to try and sell their hitherto unsold pictures. To this distinguished list were added the Yorkshiremen Copley Fielding, the watercolourist, and the young landscapist, Thomas Creswick (This last artist, when becoming a member of the Royal Academy, would jealously guard his position as the only landscape painter by blocking the selection of others - see page 54, 'Bid for Fame', Part 3).

Mr Williams felt the exhibition important enough to obtain the professional art critic William Carey, a champion of the British School, to review it.[12] Unfortunately, unlike their counterparts in Birmingham, the thrifty citizens of Worcester were not prepared to spend their money on expensive paintings. Mr Williams' catalogue shows that of the 194 paintings exhibited only thirty-two were sold to the value of £171.6s. and of these, only one sold for over 10 guineas.[13] In spite of its financial failure the promoters must have been sufficiently satisfied because similar exhibitions were held in the following two summers and again in 1838. It is interesting to note that John Constable was the only Royal Academician represented in 1835 despite having both his paintings returned unsold the previous year.[14]

Nearly seventy years after Constable exhibited in Worcester Benjamin told Lord Windsor, who was preparing his book on Constable, that the artist had left three paintings at the Williams family home asking his father:

> . . . to hang them in his dining room for a time, he
> (Constable) not having room in his house in town for
> them. My father copied an upright picture of a water-
> mill,[15] and on Constable's second visit to Worcester
> he took the copy away with him, saying he would work
> on it. It was never returned, Constable dying shortly
> afterwards. My father I can recollect saying to me,
> " Mark my words, Ben, that copy will be sold for an
> original one day"; so it was! I saw it some years ago
> exhibited with a number of Constable's works at the
> Grosvenor Gallery, having "John Constable, RA" on the
> frame. I have in my possession a picture of my father's
> painting of Hallow Park, near Worcester, on which
> Constable painted, introducing a glimpse of the River
> Severn; he also worked upon the distance.[16]

Mr Williams exhibited a painting in the 1835 exhibition titled 'Worcester from Hallow', No.162.[17] This work, now lost,[18] could be the one Constable worked on. Benjamin's other later memory of Constable was a more personal recollection. He recalled Constable's kind affection towards himself and his brothers and sisters and their calling him '"Mr. Dunstable", associating him in our childish minds with our Dunstable straw hats'.[19]

The above reminiscences must be taken with a considerable degree of caution as Leader was only four years old when Constable visited Worcester in October 1835. There is no record of him returning for the second visit and he died in 1837. The purpose of Constable's visit was to deliver three lectures on the History of Landscape Paintings at the Athenaeum, and whilst in Worcester he stayed at Bromwich Villa as a guest of Mr Williams. At sometime between July 1832 and April 1834 the family had moved across to the west bank of the River Severn to Bromwich Lane in the, then, rural parish of St John's. From Constable's correspondence at the time we learn he was reluctant to go to Worcester and wished he could get out of the commitment. But if he did not go he considered they would think him 'shabby or a charlatan'.[20] On his return he wrote that the societies there to promote intellect:

> . . . are paralysed and chilled by the drones of the
> Cathedral. It is so in all cathedral towns . . . My rambles are
> in ruin – Worcester was a sad long distance.[21]

Although Benjamin would have been too young to have been influenced by Constable himself at the time, later, when he had become a professional artist we learn from his Diaries that he was a great admirer of Constable's landscapes. Sometimes, when one of his own paintings was finished to his satisfaction, he would write 'I would not object to have it hanging next to a Constable'.[22] He kept close to hand the complete set of Lucas' engravings of Constable's 'English Landscapes', published 1830, originally a gift from Constable to Mr Williams, acknowledging they were a great influence upon his work.[23] He also believed he had, as a landscape artist, at least one thing in common with Constable, the belated official recognition accorded to them both by the most prestigious institution of British Art – The Royal Academy (Diary, 8 November, 1889. See also page 77, 'Recognition and Success').

It is most certain that his father's admiration for the 'Master' was communicated to the son through his own paintings 'after Constable' executed in his spare time, although none of Mr Williams' paintings have yet come to light. According to Benjamin, talking to Fredrick Dolman in 1897,[24] his father was fond of sketching from nature in his leisure time, especially along the banks of the Severn. On many occasions, as a young boy, Benjamin would accompany him and 'would sometimes take advantage of his father's absence from the easel and add his own touches to the canvas'.[25] If this were true one could add that it was also the beginning of Benjamin's lifetime love of painting views along the Severn.

The artist also recalled his first attempt at drawing was when he was laid up for six weeks with a broken leg:

> I was given a colour-box, and the first picture I ever
> made was a copy of an engraving of a missionary's
> hut in Jamaica - not altogether an inspiring subject.[26]

It was not, however, Mr Williams' initial wish that his son should become an artist; his intention was that Benjamin should enter his own adopted profession. By 1835 Mr Williams, was calling himself an engineer.[27] During that year he had successfully convinced his fellow citizens, by demonstrating with models and plans he had made, that it was possible to make the River Severn navigable, from Gloucester to Stourport, by means of a series of locks and weirs, for vessels drawing twelve feet of water. (Worcester already had a thriving economy due to its position on the River Severn - one of England's major 'highways' for manufactured goods to and from the Midlands and the port of Bristol. But the river was tidal, prone to severe flooding in winter, low water levels in summer and silting up which constricted the size of vessels and reliable transportation.) A navigation company was formed and Mr Williams appointed its resident engineer.[28] The initial plans were defeated in Parliament in 1837 due to opposition from the citizens of Gloucester.[29] Nevertheless, although it proved unsuccessful, a compromise solution was reached,[30] and in place of the original company The Severn Navigational Commission was set up in 1842 with Mr Williams retaining his office as resident engineer.

Other civic milestones for Mr Williams included adoption of his plans, in 1840, for widening the Worcester bridge[31] and giving evidence before a Parliamentary Select Committee in May 1845 - at the time of the railway mania - concerning proposed routes to Worcester by the Great Western and the London and North Western Railways. As a member of the Worcester Town Council he proposed an enquiry into the Corn Laws in opposition to total repeal. On his appointment as city surveyor in 1849, under the Public Health Act, he prepared plans for the improved drainage and water supply of Worcester. Although these plans were adopted by the Council strong opposition to them in the city, and the Act in general, meant they were not implemented. In conjunction with this scheme a book was published by Mr Williams entitled 'On Land Drainage and Irrigation and on the Application of Drainage water as a motive power to machinery for Agricultural Purposes'.[32]

By this time, around 1846, the family has moved again, returning back across the river to Diglis House[33] (see page 14) on the banks of the Severn just below the Cathedral in the parish of St Peter's. This was, and still is, a substantial house befitting a man, and his large family, who had risen from humble beginnings to become, both professionally and socially, a valued and respected resident of Worcester. Through his public services it was also inevitable that Mr Williams had become well-known beyond the borders of Worcestershire, a factor which no doubt further enhanced his own professional and social status and that of his family. Certainly his father's connections were invaluable to Benjamin when embarking on his artistic career. However, as mentioned earlier, Benjamin was originally destined to work with his father and was educated accordingly. As Lewis Lusk related in 1901,[34] at first this included attendance at the Worcester Royal Grammar School.[35] (The other main school in Worcester was The King's School. This was considered to be a school where the 'classics' predominated in preparation for university, whereas the Grammar School was attended by the sons of men in business and trade). A few years later, the artist himself stated that he had attended the school from the age of ten for four years and the only classes he cared about were the drawing classes.[36] Although there is no evidence to substantiate the claim that Benjamin attended the Grammar School,[37] which was then badly conducted, almost of charity status and housed in a dark and gloomy room adjoining St Swithins Church, it has been established that in 1843 at the age of twelve he was studying at the Silver Street Academy, referred to as a 'Gents' Academy'.[38]

On leaving school, in 1845, Benjamin, following in his brother Edward's footsteps, entered his father's office to learn engineering but, from the first, sketching in the field was far more to his taste than making plans and sections of locks and weirs. There were compensations though for the artist. It was part of his duties, once a week, to visit the locks between Stourport and Gloucester, in a small steam launch, paying the wages of the lock-keepers and inspecting the works. Those days on the Severn implanted a love of river scenery into the young man which grew and was translated, when he was a professional artist, into some of his best landscapes. The deciding factor behind his choosing to devote his life to art was recorded. Benjamin, in accordance to his father's wishes, entered an open competition to design a new bridge over the Severn at Upton on Severn; the old one had been washed away. It was agreed that if he failed to secure an award in the competition he should give up engineering as a career and become a painter. His plans were unplaced, and with the permission of, and financial support from, his father he was given a year to prove he had the ability to become a professional artist.[39]

At this point it must be mentioned that at some time Benjamin was a clerk at the bank of Farley, Lavender, and Owen in Worcester. This was recorded in his Diary, in the entry for 17 December, 1857, after he heard that the Bank had failed. He could have been with the Bank after leaving his father's office, but according to the artist, he occupied his days by sketching and drawing from nature. In the evenings he attended the Worcester School of Design, one of the foundation students, drawing from the antique. In 1853 he submitted a drawing entitled the 'Dancing Faun', which he had made at the school, to the Academy in London as a specimen of work for his admission as probationer to the Royal Academy Schools (There is no record of this drawing at the Academy).[40] Benjamin was accepted by the Schools on 24 December, 1853, at the age of twenty-two, and was given three months to make three drawings – a full length figure from a cast, an anatomical figure, and a skeleton. These were completed in a month and Benjamin was admitted as a student and so founded his lifelong profession. Again, there is no record of his attendance at the Academy Schools[41] but this, perhaps, can be partly explained by the artist himself. He said he:

> . . . never availed himself of the privilege as . . .[he] . . .
> had made up his mind to be a landscape painter or
> nothing else.[42]

Diglis House Hotel.
Photograph: J. Seymour,
Diglis House Hotel, Worcester.

Colour Plate 1. *The Artist's Early Studio. 8 x 12in (20.5 x 30.5cm) board.* Private Collection. Photograph: R. Cotton.

This statement is not quite true because at the beginning of his career, in the 1850s, he was painting rustic genre scenes. It is possible that Benjamin did not care for the Schools' emphasis on the all important human figure and did not feel he required the discipline designed for students younger than himself. His self-confidence must have been enhanced when, in his first year, he was lucky enough to have a picture hung and sold in the 1854 Royal Academy's Summer Exhibition.[43] The painting 'Cottage Children Blowing Bubbles', No.184, was purchased by an American, a Mr Currie, from Philadelphia for £50, a large and encouraging price for an unknown artist's work. Describing how he painted his first Academy picture, he said:

> I selected an old Worcestershire cottage with some
> children playing in the foreground. In order to
> make studies for every detail I used to walk to a
> village three miles from our house to sketch the
> cottage which I had selected to use. In the same way
> I made careful studies for the trees in the background,
> and used my younger brothers and sisters as models
> for the children.[44]

The studies and sketches were probably worked up into the finished painting in an unused coach-house (Colour Plate 1) which Benjamin converted into a studio by having a sky-light put in. (His first studio was a hayloft over the stables at Diglis House). Looking through Benjamin's early Records of Paintings Sold (between 1850 and 1856), one can conclude that, from the outset of his career, he must have been encouraged by having not only support from leading Worcester citizens, but also from other more established artists, provincial art dealers and art societies. His Records list as customers professional Worcester men such as H.J. Aldrich (Bank Manager); S.M. Beale (Solicitor); H.D. Carden (Surgeon); C.C.N. Griffiths (Draper, Hosier and Haberdasher); E. Webb (Hair Seating Manufacturer), and Henry Whiting, his mother's brother, who was a dealer in waterproof articles. It may

Possibly a pencil sketch for *'Cottage Children Blowing Bubbles'*. Private Collection.

be no coincidence that, with the exception of Beale, these men, as well as Benjamin's father, were on the committee of the Worcester Society of Arts, founded in 1853. The purpose of founding such a society was, they announced, to promote and hold periodical exhibitions of Fine Arts in the city and, with the funds or profits to buy works of art and books to form the basis of a future permanent collection in a Gallery of Art.[45] These almost annual exhibitions, to which Benjamin usually submitted work, were held from 1854 until 1865.[46] 'A View of Frog Lane' was exhibited at the first exhibition and purchased by the surgeon, Carden, for £12. A painting of this title was reproduced as an illustration in *The Art Annual*, 1901, page 15. It depicts, in the, then, house-lined cobbled lane behind the family home, Diglis House, two smocked children (disproportionately large in relation to their surroundings) carrying a loaf of bread and a can of milk.

Other customers outside his home town included Mr Thomas Underwood of Birmingham, an engraver and writer on art and archaeology.[47] From 1856 Underwood purchased a number of the young artist's paintings which were probably sold at his gallery. One of the first acquistions was 'Mending the Bird Cage' (Colour Plate 2), which is still signed B. Williams. (The majority of the artist's early works were re-signed 'B.W. Leader' at a later date). As in 'A View of Frog Lane' the young artist is still grappling with the rules of proportion and perspective. For example, the figures in the uneven paved yard, the young woman observing the man who is seated on a box repairing the bird cage, are dwarfed by the thatched dwelling. More confidence, however, is shown in the artist's handling of light and shade and attention to detail which gives the scene an overall cohesion. A noticeable feature in this painting, and other known early works, is that the sky only occupies a small proportion of the canvas. It is only when the artist begins to paint pure landscape, working in front of his subject, that the sky gains greater significance both in occupying a greater proportion of the canvas and in the artist's ability to encapsulate, over the total scene, natural light effects produced by differing weather conditions.

Another important purchaser was the Glasgow Art Union. Art Unions had sprung up since the 1830s with the objective of distributing sums of money to be spent on modern British art, to support rising talent and to educate the public's taste in art. Funds were raised by annual lotteries. Membership, in the case of the London Art Union, was one guinea per year and for that the subscriber was issued one lottery ticket. The winners could then choose a work of art of a particular value (or more if added to from their own pocket) from an approved exhibition or receive one chosen by the Society itself. Those purchased from Benjamin by the Glasgow Art Union would have been given out as prizes. They purchased five pictures in 1855 and 'Temptation' (Colour Plate 6, page 21) exhibited at the National Institute in London, No.461, in 1858. Beside giving paintings as prizes these Unions also purchased works specifically for engraving which were then distributed as 'consolation' prizes to subscribers. A later painting by Benjamin, 'Streatley on Thames' of 1887, was specifically purchased for this purpose by the London Art Union.[48]

In addition to exhibiting in his home town and at the Royal Academy in London, Benjamin sought out other venues, at this early period, to market his work. In London his name appears in the catalogues of the National Institute and the British Institution. He also submitted paintings to the Birmingham Society of Artists, Liverpool Academy and Glasgow. A painting exhibited at Birmingham in 1856 'Going to Market' was purchased by the landscape artist, Frederick William Hulme, 1816-1884. Then, like today, it was not unusual for an artist to spread his work around in order to obtain as wide a recognition as possible. Interest in the Arts in the provinces resulted in the formation of societies for holding exhibitions. These were forums for both unknown and established artists, the latter having nothing to lose by submitting their unsold work. For unknown artists they were often the only market outlet until acquiring the patronage of one or more art dealers. Gone were the days when artists could rely on the patronage of noblemen and monarchy or employment in the studio of a 'master'.

Colour Plate 2. *Mending the Bird Cage. Signed B. Williams and dated 1856. 20 x 17in (51 x 43cm).* Private Collection.

This was a time of experimentation for Benjamin as it would be for any artist at the outset of his career trying to assert his own individual identity. He was looking to the old masters and painting pictures after the style of the landscapists such as John Crome, Richard Wilson, Willis[49] and Thomas Woodward. The current popularity for rustic subjects depicting children at play and wearing smocks (Plate 3 and Colour Plate 6), cottage interiors (Colour Plate 4) and exteriors (Colour Plate 2) would have been noted by the young artist in the work of William Hemsley (fl.1848-1893) and members of the Cranbrook Colony such as Thomas Webster (1800-1886) and Frederick Daniel Hardy (1826-1912). He also absorbed the style of the established contemporary artists, especially the members of the Pre-Raphaelite Brotherhood and their followers. Although the Brotherhood had already disbanded by the time Benjamin was exhibiting at the Royal Academy they were still very much in the news and influenced the way the younger artists painted. Works by Benjamin painted during this early period, and some of the titles given to them, suggest that he was undecided which branch of painting to pursue - figure or landscape. 'The Chair Mender' of 1856, (Plate 3), 'The Young Mother', 1856, (Colour Plate 4) and 'Landscape', 1855, (Colour Plate 5) are examples of his early work. All three paintings show that the artist was influenced by the Pre-Raphaelite style, especially that of Millais, in the careful attention paid to the depiction of detail. But one has to take into account that the detail of his work was also the result of his training in draughtsmanship and the precision which was necessary to prepare engineering plans in his father's office.

'The Chair Mender' (Plate 3) was exhibited in 1856, first at Worcester then at Birmingham and Liverpool where it was finally sold for £12. When it was later re-exhibited at the 1882 Worcester Society of Arts Exhibition the catalogue stated it was loaned by Richard Smith-Carington who was then married to one of Benjamin's younger sisters, Maria Patty. Smith-Carington had inherited his father's nursery business, established a worldwide seed business and had become renowned for introducing the Worcester Pearmain apple.

The painting was executed on the artist's 'door-step' and is a genre scene set against a topographical view of a part of Worcester. Diglis House, the family home, is out of picture but it was situated opposite the fisherman's cottage depicted in the painting. This cottage once stood at the bottom of Severn Street where it came out onto the tow path. (The tow path was made in the 1840s by sinking old trows and canal boats, filled with stone, after Mr Williams Senior had built his locks and weirs). Other identifiable features are the Canon's House which stands in the Cathedral grounds behind the stone wall abounding the tow path, and the Old Dean's Palace in the middle distance. St Andrew's Spire, know as the 'Glover's Needle', dominates the skyline. To its left are the buildings then owned by Gascoine's Seed Merchants and Stella's Brewers. The chair mender sits on his box repairing a rush seat. Materials of his trade, a bundle of rushes, lie on the ground by him. From the state of his hob- nailed boots and torn, muddied trouser bottoms he was probably a 'traveller' who plied his craft from door to door. However, in a letter dated 22 July, 1912, the artist recalled that 'The seated man was I think a fisherman of the name of Jenkins'.[50] Confirming the locality of the scene he added that the elder of the two girls watching the man work was posed for by his sister Sally.[51] Beyond the main figures, along the tow path, smaller figures go about their business and an abandoned. wooden paddle for a fisherman's boat rests on a wicker basket. Even at this early stage of his career Benjamin has employed artistic licence and compositional perspective devices which, as we shall see, were later used with greater sophistication as he gained more confidence. Patches of light colour or white are used to draw attention to focal points and to lead the eye diagonally into the pictorial distance (see also Colour Plate 2). Reflections in the water add spatial depth to the scene. In reality the spire is more to the right but the artist has placed it so as to give a more balanced composition. The awkwardness in the painting is because the figures sit rather uncomfortably in their setting (see also Colour Plate 2). The chair mender is far too big, in relation to the cottage behind, and his legs are too long.

In 'The Young Mother' (Colour Plate 4, page 20) we also find the elongation of limbs. This

Plate 3. *The Chair Mender.*
Signed and dated 1856.
18 x 24in (45.5.x 61cm).
Private Collection.
Photograph: Courtesy of
Agnew's, London.

painting was exhibited at the Royal Academy in 1856, No.718, and at Worcester the same year, No.205. Unsold, the painting remained in the artist's possession during his lifetime. When first exhibited it carried with it a long quotation from Thomas Campbell's poem 'Pleasures of Hope'.[52] It was not unusual for Victorian artists to append quotes from poems which were seen to be relevant to the subject matter of their paintings. It taught the public to equate painting with literature – something to be read, like a poem or novel, in rectangular format. This interior cottage scene of a pretty young mother, neatly groomed and wearing a brilliant turquoise gown, sitting next to the cradle containing her child conveys a sentiment of rustic contentment. This is the way urban exhibition-goers preferred to see rural life depicted, rather than reality, where the change from an agricultural-based society to an industrialised one had brought great poverty to rural areas. In spite of the artist's inadequate grasp of perspective, in the depiction of the staircase for example, a great deal of attention has been paid to the detail of the crude brick and wooden interior with its floor patched with stone slabs, the blackened hearth with the kettle over the fire and bellows hanging nearby, and a cat warming itself. The style of the quilt over the baby in the cane rocking cradle is typical of old Warwickshire quilting. Precedents for such Victorian domestic genre scenes as this were the Dutch paintings of the seventeenth century. They would have been seen at loan exhibitions of old masters, especially those organized by the British Institute[53] in London to give students the opportunity to copy such works.

The unidentifiable 'Landscape' (Colour Plate 5, page 20), painted the year before in 1855, is less successful than the genre scenes. It appears as if it were painted from a tinted photograph rather than in front of nature. Whilst it was still the traditional practice for an artist to paint his finished landscape in the studio from sketches and studies done on the spot, (even photographs were used as artistic aids from the mid-nineteenth century) there was a growing call, especially from the art critics, to revitalise English landscape art by recording nature in a direct and realistic manner without any concessions to picturesque landscape conventions derived from

Colour Plate 4. *The Young Mother. Signed and dated 1856. 18 x 24in (45.5 x 61cm).*
Private Collection. Photograph: Courtesy of Richard Green Gallery, London.

Colour Plate 5.
Landscape. Signed and dated 1855. 15 x 21¼in (38 x 55.5cm).
Reproduced by kind permission of Sefton MBC Leisure Services Department, Arts and Cultural Services, Atkinson Art Gallery.

Colour Plate 10. *A Quiet Valley Amongst the Welsh Hills. Signed and dated 1860. 28 x 42¼in (71 x 108.5cm).* Photograph: R. Cotton. Reproduced by permission of Worcester City Museum and Art Gallery.

Pencil drawing (from an album) for A Quiet Valley. Photograph: Victoria and Albert Picture Library.

Quiet Valley among the Welsh Hills' with a painting called 'Val d'Aosta', 1858, by a contemporary landscape artist, John Brett (1830-1902), who fell under the direct influence of Ruskin and the Pre-Raphaelites. Brett's painting was exhibited at the Royal Academy in 1858 and Leader must have noted the high viewpoint looking down and across the valley to the mountains, the great attention to detail, and the praise accorded to it by Ruskin because his own painting is a direct reference to it. Leader takes a similar viewpoint and exhibits the same attention to detail and luminosity. No artist is 'an island', especially at the beginning of his career. Aspiring artists gather material not only from popular locations frequented by other artists but also from looking at what, and how, 'masters' have painted in the past as well as at contemporary artists' works in current exhibitions. 'A Quiet Valley among the Welsh Hills' was also exhibited at the Royal Academy, but not until 1860, No. 467, and was purchased by a Worcester citizen, Charles Wheeley Lea (brother of John Lea, partner with Perrins of the Worcestershire sauce fame). It is now in the collection of the Worcester City Art Gallery, donated by Mrs Wheeley-Lea after her husband's death.

Charles Wheeley Lea, or Chas Lea as Leader called him, was also one of the instigators in setting up a public subscription among the citizens of Worcester to purchase another Welsh scene, 'On the Hills above Bettws-y-coed',* 1861 (Colour Plate 11, page 32). The other person responsible was Edward Evans, one of the founders of the Worcester City and County Bank, the Worcester Chamber of Commerce and the Vinegar Works in Worcester. The painting was presented to the Worcester Society of Arts. Like the previous Welsh scene, 'A Quiet Valley among the Welsh Hills', it is painted in the same manner. The artist's viewpoint was from Clogwyn Gyrau, high above the village, looking along the Llugwy valley to Capel Curig with Moel Siabod in the distance. Unfortunately, the distinctive crags and slopes in this area, which were prominent in Leader's day and featured in so many Victorian Welsh landscapes, are now obscured by conifer plantations.[26] The figures no longer play a dominant role within the scene.

At an exhibition of Leader's paintings held in the Worcester City Art Gallery in 1991 visitors were asked to comment on why Leader had included the two figures in 'On the Hills above Bettws-y-coed'. Their varied responses included – 'the figures being there as compositional devices to lead one's eye into the landscape diagonally from the left foreground'; 'to balance the two fir trees'; 'to show the immense vastness and scale of the view'; 'to give colour and form to the landscape'. It was also thought they were placed there to give a human involvement to the landscape or to depict the idyllic life-style of the peasants when in reality country life was harsh. Placing small figures in landscape as compositional devices has been frequently employed in the tradition of landscape painting. Constable used this device and his figures were usually accompanied by a 'collie dog'. In 'On the Hills above Bettws-y-coed' Leader has borrowed the 'dog' (it is also in the 1860 Welsh scene) as well as the Constable small patches of red, mostly on clothing, and the white highlights, as focal points leading one's eye into the pictorial space. These type of devices were to be used time and again in a great many of Leader's future landscapes.

Leader's Sales Records show that another prominent Worcester citizen had purchased one of his paintings at this time. A.C. Sheriff, MP for Worcester, acquired a Scottish landscape 'The Rocky Bed of a Mountain Burn', in 1859. In this same year two of Leader's Royal Academy exhibits attracted the attention of Academicians. David Roberts RA (1796-1864), painter of architectural subjects, purchased 'A Quiet Pool in Glen Fallock', 1859, No.933 and the London genre and historical genre artist, Alfred Elmore RA (1815-1881) purchased 'A Sketch on a Common', 1859, No.16.

Another artist, the landscape painter Frederick William Hulme (1816-1884), should also be mentioned at this point. (He had earlier, in 1856, purchased a painting by Leader.) It is believed that Hulme and Leader collaborated on a painting titled 'Sweet Summertime'[27] which is dated 1860. The work was not recorded by Leader unlike an earlier small picture, 'A View of Frog Lane', he mentioned in his Sales Records for 1854, as painted by 'Ed Evans and self' and sold to the Worcester surgeon, Carden. It was not unusual for Victorian artists to collaborate on paintings. Thomas Sidney Cooper (1803-1902) painted cattle and other animals in the landscapes of a number of artists' works including Frederick Richard Lee and Thomas Creswick. Creswick also worked with other artists, in addition to Cooper, including William Powell Frith RA (1819-1909). Their painting was exhibited at the 1853 Royal Academy exhibition, No.375, titled 'The Happy Springtime'. An older artist, William Shayer (1787-1879) sometimes collaborated with Edward, the father of the Williams family of painters.

Leader's paintings were now beginning to be noticed by the London-based art dealers, of whom two would play important roles in establishing the artist's reputation through the promotion of his work. Art dealers had been operating in England since the eighteenth

* Note earlier form of spelling of 'Bettws-y-coed'.

century, if not earlier, although those who first dealt in paintings were usually framers, sellers of art materials, printers and engravers who also sold artists' works in their shops. By the time Leader had embarked on his artistic career a professional art dealership market had emerged which was thriving and multiplying to meet the demand of the new class of art collector. Throughout the eighteenth century and up until about the time of Lord Egremont's death in 1837 art patronage was dominated by the land-owning aristocracy. But with vast wealth, one attribute of the Industrial Revolution, concentrated in the hands of a new middle class, located mainly in the Midlands and North of England, a shift in patronage occurred.

The new patrons were the men in industry and commerce - bankers and brewers, merchants and manufacturers. They did not want dubious old masters from the Continent and portraits hanging on the drawing-room walls of their newly acquired mansions, preferring instead contemporary paintings signed by British artists. They had a preference for subject-paintings because they mirrored middle-class life or values and, as townsmen with a nostalgia for the 'good old' English countryside, they also liked rural genre scenes depicting country life as happy and contented and landscapes that, according to the industralist, Mr Millbank, in Benjamin Disraeli's novel 'Coningsby', published in 1844, 'gave him the broad plains, the green lanes, and running streams of his own land'.[28] These types of paintings would have been pleasant reminders of holiday excursions away from the burgeoning industrial cities, not of the reality of the countryside with its poverty and unrest brought about by the Industrial Revolution. Such pictures would have pricked their conscience or represented a threat to the comfortable position in society they had made for themselves.

These new collectors, often untutored, but conscious of the social importance of art, depended on the dealers as knowledgeable intermediaries. The dealers in turn 'courted' their *nouveaux riches* clients by inviting them to their galleries for a private preview of paintings, purchased from artists, to be exhibited at that year's Royal Academy Summer Exhibition. The client offered such a painting would be aware of the prestige to himself in owning an exhibit at one of the main events on the London social calendar, an event which was reported nationally in all the major newspapers, journals, and magazines. Its importance drew not just the London-based public but also those living further afield. One such frequent visitor was the Reverend Francis Kilvert who travelled from Clyro in Radnorshire. His (Kilvert's) Diaries reveal his preferred subject-matter to be those paintings depicting the rather titillating female form.[29]

Leader, also, found it preferable to avail himself of the dealers' services as, in their role as 'agent', they had the expertise to promote and market his paintings. As he became more popular and the demand for his landscapes grew he most probably found it more profitable and less tedious to sell to dealers by the lot than to cater personally for collectors. One of the most influential and respected London-based art dealers in the second half of the nineteenth century was Messrs. Agnew's, a family company which had its origins in Manchester earlier in the century. Both Creswick's and Linnell's landscapes had passed through its hands and, by the time interest was shown in Leader, Agnew's was about to open a London branch. William Agnew first bought two of Leader's paintings in 1859. He purchased a small upright picture 'A Chat by the Way', exhibited at the Royal Academy, No.522, for £15 and, later in the year, Leader recorded in his Diary (2 October) painting an upright with the title 'Fishing in North Wales', a view on the Lluwgy, for 'Mr. Agnew-Manchester' which was sold for £50.

In 1859, Thomas Wallis, another respected London-based art dealer, also began to buy paintings from Leader. The first picture he purchased was a Welsh scene, 'On the Llugwy, near Capel Curig', when it was exhibited at the Worcester Society of Arts, No.937. Unlike Leader's business relationship with Agnew's, the artist, according to later Diary entries, formed a close friendship with 'Tom' Wallis, often staying at the dealer's home in London and entertaining Wallis' daughters when they visited his sisters in Worcester. Leader first exhibited at Wallis' exhibitions, held at Suffolk Street in London, during the first half of the 1860s. When the dealer moved to the French Gallery, 120 Pall Mall Street in 1866, Leader became a regular exhibitor at Wallis' annual Winter Exhibitions (from November to January) comprised of cabinet paintings by Continental (mainly French) and British artists. Recognizing Leader's

Colour Plate 11.
On the Hills above Bettws-y-coed.
Signed and dated 1861. 35⅜ x
52¾in (90 x 134cm).
Photograph: R. Cotton.
Reproduced by permission of
Worcester City Museum and Art
Gallery.

artistic potential Wallis was the first major art dealer actively to promote Leader's paintings and advise him on what, or what not, to submit to the London and Paris venues. Wallis also promoted the work of two other aspiring artists in London, both contemporaries of Leader, the Scottish painters William Quiller Orchardson (1832-1910) and John Pettie (1839-1893).

Leader at this time also made the acquaintance of another man who would also become of great value to him - Samuel Carter Hall. Leader had dined with Hall in Worcester on two occasions, first at the home of the bank manager Henry J. Aldrich and then at W.H. Kerr's, a partner of R.W. Binns, owners of the Porcelain Digilis Factory in Worcester. As a consequence of these meetings Hall, probably noting the potential of the young artist, invited Leader to call on him when in Town (24 November, 1858). Before meeting Leader, Hall already had the reputation of actively supporting and encouraging British artists through his proprietorship of *The Art Union Monthly Journal,* renamed *The Art Journal* in 1849. Hall's campaign for British art collectors to buy British included the exposure of the importation of phoney old masters from the Continent. *The Art Journal* was also the mouthpiece of the several art unions around Britain. As mentioned above, many young artists like Leader benefited from their patronage. *The Art Journal,* under the editorship of Hall and its publisher, James Virtue, would become the most consistent promoter of Leader's paintings, favourably reviewing them during the sixties and seventies.

Leader's work caught the eye of another publisher, Herbert Ingram, founder of the *Illustrated London News.*[30] He purchased the artist's painting 'Early Summer Time' in 1859 and had it reproduced as a colour print in the paper's 2 June 1860 Supplement.[31] It is believed this was the first time one of Leader's paintings was reproduced for a journal and the proprietor's praise was unreserved. This Surrey pastoral scene in the vicinity of Albury village was seen to be a 'truly English bit of landscape under a truly English May sky, chequered with clouds with enough freshness in the air to render exercise agreeable'. Represented thus by the artist 'who, in the composition and treatment of his subject, shows himself possessed of the soul to enjoy Nature in her gladdest and grandest mood'.[32]

In spite of the growing number of private commissions, the interest shown by dealers, and increased sales, Leader still expressed doubts about the manner in which he painted during this period and felt the need to search for new subjects. This restlessness seemed also to be reflected in his personal life. It was a time of finding a niche, the right one, for himself and wanting to be independent. During the autumn of 1859, after returning from Capel Curig where he had spent the summer, he took up lodgings with his younger brother Alfred just outside Worcester at Bank House, Whittington the home of a Mrs Doe. Perhaps he felt there was not enough room to work at his family home at Diglis House and if he was already working in a disciplined manner, as he was to do later, disliking interruptions, he may have found the family environment too disruptive - there were still four brothers and four sisters living at home. Mrs Doe's husband, Thomas Enoch, was one of the picture dealers mentioned above. In addition to being a carver, gilder, print-seller and colour-man, with a shop at 42 High Street,

Colour Plate 12. *The Outskirts of a Farm. Signed and dated 1860. 29 x 39½in (73.5 x 100.5cm).* Private Collection. Photograph: George Bushell.

Worcester, he also bought a number of Leader's small paintings from 1859 to 1873.

An almost square picture titled 'The Outskirts of a Farm', 1860 (Colour Plate 12) shows how rural Whittington was a century and a half ago with sheep lying about and hens, chicks and turkeys scratching, in a lane bordered on the right by a sandy bank lined with trees and on the left by timber-beamed farm buildings, probably part of Church Farm. As indicated by the greenness of the leaves and very little shadow, the time and season seems to be around midday in early summer, the time and season the Pre-Raphaelites frequently opted for with their passion for visual and expressionist clarity.

Leader also felt living so far from London in Worcestershire was an impediment to his future prospects. What was needed was a base, and studio, at the centre of the art world. An opportunity to achieve this arose through his acquaintance with one Serjeant Thomas, a lawyer whose profession took him on the circuit to Worcester. The latter's interest in art, and presumbly the profits to be made from dealing, led him to give up the Bar and turn picture dealer. His encouragement to Leader not only included the purchase of a number of the latter's paintings at the end of 1859 and during 1860, but also the renting to the artist of his chambers at Serjeant's Inn, Chancery Lane, for which he had no further use. According to Leader's Diary he took the chambers, using them as a studio, for only a short while in 1861, whilst lodging with his eldest sister Sarah in Camden Town, as they had to be given up a year later when Thomas died.

Residing in London presented Leader with the additional opportunity of greater social intercourse with fellow artists more familar with the capital's art scene. He became a member of the Langham Sketching Club,[33] an offshoot of the Artist's Society founded 1830, situated in the Langham Chambers, Portland Place.[34] George Vicat Cole was already a member as were many London based artists such as Charles Cattermole RI, RBA (1832-1900); Frederick

Colour Plate 13. *A Fisherman's Haunt. Signed and dated 1864. 31½ x 51in (80 x 129.5cm).* Private Collection. Photograph: Courtesy of Christie's.

Weeks (fl.1854–1893); George Goodwin Kilburn RI, RBA (1839-1924), and John Anster Fitzgerald (1832-1906). In addition to the Club's congenial suppers, there were Friday study evenings between October and May at which members had two hours to produce an illustration, in their choice of medium, of a set predetermined subject. No models or aids were provided for the carrying out of the idea suggested and when the two hours were up, finished or unfinished it was then exhibited with the others for comment. There was also special conversazione just before 'sending-in day', at which members show their pictures before forwarding them to the Royal Academy to be either accepted or rejected. Whilst a few pictures went on to become famous, for many it was their only 'show'. Unfortunately it is not known whether Leader ever subjected his proposed Royal Academy pictures for their first 'public' criticism or that he participated in the study evenings. He certainly did not attend the Club regularly during this early period in his career because, according to his Diary, during the last five or six months of 1861 he was back at Mrs Doe's in Whittington with a foot inflammation, which he said almost led to the loss of the foot (Diary, 8 January, 1862). Whittington from this time would be Leader's home until he moved to Surrey in 1889.

There were only three Diary entries for 1862, in January and February. In two of these Leader mentions a painting (Colour Plate 13) which he was very proud of, believing it was better than anything he had ever exhibited before in London (Diary, 18 February). While working on it he called it 'The Fisherman's Home' but it was renamed 'A Fisherman's Haunt' when exhibited at the British Institution the same year, No.511. Leader's viewpoint was from a meadow (now a disused wharf) opposite the Redstone Rock just below Stourport on the River Severn looking towards Worcester. Leader's own words aptly describe the scene:

> . . . It is a scene on an unusual channel of the Severn near
> Stourport. An old man had a mongrel kind of craft anchored
> there. He used to live aboard; did so for years. The boat was
> very picturesque with nets and fishing implements about
> it. So I have painted it and it makes rather an original
> subject . . . (Diary, 8 January)

In spite of its interesting subject matter the painting did not sell in London nor did it later that year, when exhibited at Worcester, No.204, at a reduced price (£80 down from £100). The painting was eventually sold in 1864 to an unknown buyer for £100.

The organization of the composition is similar to that in Colour Plates 10 and 11 (pages 29 and 32) and was to be employed frequently throughout Leader's career, becoming almost a 'trade mark'. The horizon line is higher on one side of the scene than the other. The eye is led diagonally into the landscape from the left along the river to the extended vista on the lower horizon line beyond the rocky cliff. (In future paintings Leader invariably leads one into his landscapes diagonally, initially to, or past, the higher horizon focal point and then on into the distance). In addition to the use of bright prismatic colours to ensure maximum illumination and great attention to the detail of the landscape, there are the 'Constable touches' of red (the fisherman's cap) and white (the fishing nets).

Bid for Fame (Part 2)
1863-1870

There are no entries in the Diaries for two years from 19 February, 1862. On 11 February, 1864, we learn that Leader was in good health after recovering from a foot inflammation which had left him 'lame' and with a 'slight limp'. His career also seemed to be in a healthy position as he noted on the same day that he was 'successful in his profession selling every picture I paint and that is saying much for I painted many pictures last year'. Leader recorded forty-one pictures sold in 1863 for a total of £1,154. 2s. This was more than he had ever sold in any one previous year since beginning the records in 1850. In 1861 he had sold eighteen pictures for a total of £527.14s. 6d., and in 1862 nineteen were recorded sold for £543.12s. The 1864 sales records also show that he was selling more individual pictures for over £100. In 1861 he had sold two; in 1862 – one; in 1863 – four; and in 1864 – eight. The price per size of canvas had not risen. The figures indicate that Leader was becoming recognised as a promising landscape artist.

Although Agnew's and Wallis had shown interest in Leader's paintings, the main purchasers of his work were still, in 1863, mostly the provincial art dealers such as Tomlinson of Liverpool and Doe of Worcester. The remaining paintings were sold when exhibited at various Art institutions in London and the provinces and privately to local Worcester figures with a growing number of commissions further afield. The most prestigious sale to date for Leader, outside the art world, was in 1863 when Mr William E. Gladstone, then the Chancellor of the Exchequer, purchased his Royal Academy exhibit 'A Welsh Churchyard', No.440 for £100. (Colour Plate 14). When Gladstone sold it through Christie's Auction House on 21 June, 1875 it was purchased by Agnew's for £178.10s. and immediately resold to Charles Gassiot, a wealthy port and sherry importer and keen collector of art.[1]

Colour Plate 14 (Above).
A Welsh Churchyard.
Signed and dated 1863.
32 x 58in (81.5 x 147.5cm).
Guildhall Art Gallery, Corporation of London/Bridgeman Art Library, London.

The scene of the painting is of an area of the churchyard around the old fourteenth century church of St Michael and All Angels situated on the west bank of the River Conway in the village of Betws-y-coed, North Wales. Throughout his career Leader painted many pictures from different viewpoints of this beautiful little church and churchyard with the Conway gently flowing by: referring to 1860s material, painted on the spot, even for works dated after 1890. In this carefully composed and detailed early painting the church itself is, in reality, out of the painting on the left but one can just detect the river Conway, highlighted amid the trees in the middle distance. The sombre grey slate-topped sarcophagus tombs and the dominant dark green yew trees, which can still be seen today, make a striking contrast to the backdrop of yellow fields and hillside of Mynydd Garthmyn bathed in the late afternoon sunshine of a summer's day. It is this contrast of light and shade skilfully distributed throughout the scene, which will become the key to the effectiveness of the black and white engravings executed from the artist's paintings.

Leader was pleased with the reception of 'A Welsh Churchyard' at the Royal Academy exhibition and noted that the painting 'was universally liked and pronounced by *The Times*, and other papers, as one of the best landscapes of the season' (Diary, 11 February, 1864). Contrary to Leader's remarks concerning the newspapers' reviews of the painting in the Royal Academy's Exhibition, research has only uncovered one brief mention by *The Art Journal* art critic stating that the landscape 'shows some careful studies of yew trees watching, as it were, like mourners among the tombs'.[2] This was written under the heading 'The Royal Academy Exhibition; Landscape Schools Old and New'. The reviewer had included Leader in what he believed was an emerging 'new' school of British landscape painting, in which were the artists George Vicat Cole, Frederick William Hulme, Andrew McCallum (1821-1902) and George Sant (fl.1856-1877). These artists, the reviewer wrote, represented a 'new school of detail, free in great measure from the eccentricity and extravagance of earlier years, . . . of out-door study'. What was meant here was that these artists were seen attempting to capture in paint the natural effects of nature – of light, colour, mood and atmosphere – instead of just recording facts. The impetus to record facts, rather than effects, was seen to have led to 'eccentricity' and 'extravagance' by those artists of the Pre-Raphaelite School. *The Art Journal* critic also named those artists he thought comprised the 'old school' and these were the Royal Academicians Thomas Creswick, Richard Redgrave, David Roberts, George Jones (1786-1869), and two non-members John Linnell and James Francis Danby (1816-1875). They were all established artists of the previous generation whose paintings conveyed a very personal style and manner.

The following year, 1864, *The Art Journal* critic reviewing The Royal Academy exhibition repeated his pleasure at the Pre-Raphaelite School's demise, although he conceded that it had done a service to Art in the 'apprenticeship of genius. Devoted study of nature was the only serving truth of Pre-Raphaelism. The part Ruskin played in this shouldn't be forgotten'.[3] Other critics were writing along similar lines. Whilst acknowledging the debt to the realism of Pre-Raphaelism, Tom Taylor, writing in *The Times*, was glad that the 'exaggerated labour on the minutiae'[4] had been subdued to the extent where more attention was given to the whole. He was also encouraged to see that 'rabid medievalism . . . [and] . . . other eccentricities and extravagances of young and ardent innovators are disappearing before the recurrent tide of English common sense'.[5] *The Art Journal's* critic went further in his 1865 review of the Royal Academy's 'Ninety-Seventh Exhibition', reporting that for the first time during many years 'the English School is seen not only in its variety but in its vigour and vastness. This is due to the freedom from tyrants over life, property, thought and from nature . . . our nature school has become directly and dogmatically naturalistic'.[6] The critic went on to dismiss the Italianate landscapes of 'Poussin, Rosa, Claude, Wilson and de Loutherbourg'. Even the 'blottesque' manner of John Constable was deemed 'slovenly' and Turner was believed to be at the 'full zenith of his power'.[7] By 1867 the leading London art critics were writing of the extinction of Pre-Raphaelism in its more extreme form.

Colour Plate 15. *Autumn's Last Gleam. Signed and dated 1865. 36 x 60in (91.5 x 152.5cm).* Photograph: Courtesy of Bonhams.

Because of the success of 'A Welsh Churchyard' Leader toyed with the idea of putting his name down as a candidate for election as an Associate of the Royal Academy. The following year he was convinced he should because his 1865 Royal Academy pictures, which he painted for Alfred Castellian of Liverpool (Commissioner and General Merchant), 'Autumn's Last Gleam', No.468 (Colour Plate 15) and 'A Sunny Afternoon, North Wales', No.317 were also successes and were 'generally thought to be an advance'.

Leader's Diary for the first quarter of 1865 relates how hard he worked on the two pictures. While painting 'Autumn's Last Gleam' during February and March he called it his 'cottage picture'. It caused him much frustration because 'severe' weather had prevented Leader from going out of doors to 'paint the elm trees from Nature' which he had already sketched in on the canvas. The urgency of painting the elms was because he felt he could not continue on the painting until he had completed them. By 7 March when the painting was almost finished his father, who was the first to view it, thought it was his best work and advised his son to charge Mr Castellian a higher price than initially considered. On sending both paintings to Castellian before they went to the Royal Academy he said he 'was bold enough to ask £250 and £200 for them' instead of £220 and £135 respectively: this was the first time Leader received such large prices for his work. Millais, who was on the Hanging Committee that year having been elected Royal Academician two years previously, was suitably impressed with the paintings and told Leader that he was 'certain of being elected'.[8] *The Art Journal's* review added fuel to his hopes. After praising 'Autumn's Last Gleam',[9] they stated their belief that there was 'no man more likely to obtain early election'.[10] It could be assumed from Leader's Diary that he did put his name forward, but not having the conviction of the others believed that if he was elected then he would 'thank his lucky stars'.[11] He was not elected on this occasion and contrary to what William P. Frith RA was reported to have said, later in 1883, that Leader lost by only one vote,[12] the Royal Academy's General Assembly Election's Minutes did not record the artist's name.[13] It is only in the Election's Minutes for 31 January, 1867 that Leader's name was first forwarded for election to an Associate: then he received just one vote.[14]

For the next eighteen years Leader would have to endure feelings of disappointment and frustration at not being elected, and experience the 'ups and downs' of exhibiting as an outsider at the Royal Academy's summer exhibitions. For example, the following year, 1866, Leader's

Colour Plate 16. *A Fine Day in Autumn, North Wales. Signed and dated 1866. 28¾ x 51in (73 x 129.5cm).*
Photograph: Permission of Blackburn Museum and Art Gallery, Lancs.

Diary entry for 21 May stated that when he first saw his picture 'The Close of Summer', No.182, and 'A Fine Day in Autumn, North Wales', No.573, (Colour Plate 16) on the Royal Academy walls on varnishing day he was unhappy to find them badly hung.
They were:

> . . . hung above the line and not looking well . . . was
> disappointed with their appearance especially the
> River Scene (No.182) which was hung between two
> dark full length portraits and looked very bleak and flat
> I have not made an advance this year but yet not
> receded.[15]

'Varnishing Days' at the Royal Academy were first instituted in 1809 for members only to retouch and varnish their paintings before the opening of the Exhibition. By the time Leader was exhibiting, 'Varnishing Days' were also open to non-members, although they only had one day while members had two, a rule still in force today. For the exhibiting artists it was usually the only opportunity to meet each other; a rather relaxed and social event. On this particular 'Varnishing Day' in 1866 not only was Leader upset by the hanging of his pictures, but also because his friend and fellow landscape artist, George Vicat Cole, had his picture 'Evening Best', No.403, placed on the line and was thought (by Leader) to be much better than his own.[16]

In spite of the usual individual grievances regarding bad hanging which occurred every year, all the regular exhibiting landscape artists were usurped in 1866 by 'a new man, Graham by name, a Scotsman who has a large and powerful picture of a Highland flood that seems to attract the most attention of any landscape in this exhibition' (Diary, 21 May). The painting, a Scottish scene, was called 'Stream in Spate', No.373, by Peter Graham (1836-1921) who was making his debut at the Royal Academy. Taylor, in *The Times*, believed the landscape had successfully achieved what the majority of the other landscapes had failed to do and this was in 'its subordination of the parts to the whole and the predominance throughout of a prevailing sentiment; the Desolation of the power of the storm, and the struggle of the elements'.[17] These were seen as the leading ideas of the picture which should, according to Taylor, account for all the viewer felt before it. The landscapes by both Cole and Leader were selected, amongst others, because they were seen by Taylor as failing to convey 'a sentiment' which was the result of the insistence of detail in parts of the scene leaving the whole imperfect. 'Only a great painter. . . [implying Graham] . . . can give us the two things in due proportion'.[18] Graham's fluid style of painting would have been seen as very different from those English artists who had taken on board the literal style of the Pre-Raphaelite artists. Graham had been a pupil of the naturalistic school of Robert Scott Lauder RSA (1803-1869), in Edinburgh and, as a consequence, his landscapes depict the effects of nature. In contrast to Graham's exhibited work, Leader's highly finished 'A Fine Day in Autumn, North Wales', No.573, is heavy and still with the foreground rocks dominating the viewer's attention. The lake, probably Llyn-y-Gader, lies like a sheet of molten silver in its basin of smooth green hills and the scene conveys no sentiment.

In spite of Leader's feelings of impotency in regard to achieving academic success he must have been gratified that some of his paintings were entering important private collections. In 1866 David Price purchased 'Meeting of the Conway and Llugwy' (see Appendix 3 for other paintings by Leader owned by Price). Price's wealth, accumulated through the woollen trade, enabled him to amass a large collection of over three hundred paintings, mainly by contemporary British artists at his residence in Queen Anne Street, London.[19]

Leader was also ensuring that his chosen career was profitable. In February, 1867 he wrote that he had repurchased twenty-two of his paintings. These were from Taplin, a Worcester brewer, who had been buying from the artist since 1860. It seems that a financial crisis had made it necessary for Taplin to sell his house and effects, including the paintings by Leader. The artist offered to buy them back at the original price plus five percent for a total of £518. 3s. 9d. The offer was accepted. Leader said he hoped '. . . to do well by them. Working on them and selling them one at a time' (Diary, 23 February). His sales records show that between fifty and one hundred percent profit was made on each one. For example, Taplin purchased 'A Fisherman's Haunt- Sketch' for £5 in 1862 (this was the small oil sketch for the finished work – see Colour Plate 13, page 34). Leader resold the sketch for £10 within a month of its repurchase.

His successful business transaction was soon forgotten as he was once again preoccupied with the fate of his 1867 Royal Academy pictures. He had exhibited two Welsh landscapes that year 'An Autumn Evening in the Valley of the Lledr', No.501, and 'Through the Glen', No.528. He said he was disgusted to find the latter hung 'shamefully'. It was not only 'skied' but also, according to Leader, between 'one light and another almost white picture'. He concluded that 'the hanging this year is shameful, two figure painters and a portrait painter being the hanging committee . . . result is the landscape painters are snubbed' (Diary, 3 July, 1867). When working on this picture Leader called it the 'dark Glen'. It is a steep, dark, wooded valley scene and he had the premonition that if the painting was not hung in a favourable position it would not do it, or himself, justice (1 February). Of course, it was hung badly and the sombre landscape must have been greatly accentuated by being placed between two bright pictures high on the wall where the light would have been dim. Knowing that he would fail again to be elected he despondently noted that 'a landscape by a young man hung on the line and that is by a cousin of the President [Sir Francis Grant] who will of course be A.R.A. soon. I don't stand the Nights ! chance at the present' (3 July).

Leader's bitterness was exacerbated because he had just returned from Paris where he had seen his 1865 Royal Academy exhibit, 'Autumn's Last Gleam'[20] hung 'very favourably'[21] at the Exposition Universelle. Lent by Mr Castellian, this was the first time Leader had had a painting exhibited on the continent. While in Paris he said he 'studied the French school of landscape, took notes, and felt that . . . [he] . . . had learnt much'.[22] The school Leader referred to was most probably that of the Barbizon landscape painters. He would have seen the paintings of Charles-Francois Daubigny (1817-1878), and Jean-Baptiste-Camille Corot (1796-1875), the School's leading artists, who influenced many French landscapists including the Impressionists. There is a copy of a Corot landscape painted by Leader dated 1865 (Colour Plate 17) of which the French artist was reported to have said graciously 'that it was better than his own'.[23] Leader has managed to imitate Corot's delicate brushwork, his muted palette, and soft effects which is in marked contrast to his other exhibited works at this time.

It is not known when Leader first visited Paris. His first mention of the

Colour Plate 17. *Copy of Corot. Signed and dated 1865. 12½ x 16½in (32 x 42cm) board.*
Private Collection.

Colour Plate 18. *Derwentwater from Ladore: Morning. Signed and dated 1867. 16 x 24in (41 x 61cm) board.*
Photograph: Courtesy of Richard Green, London.

Colour Plate 19. *Derwentwater from Ladore: Morning. Signed and dated 1874. 28 x 42in (71 x 106.5cm).*
Photograph: Courtesy of Richard Green, London.

Colour Plate 20. *An Autumn Evening on the Severn, near Worcester. Signed and dated 1868. 29½ x 47½in (75 x 120.5cm).* Photograph: Courtesy of Richard Green, London.

city was after his return from a round trip to 'France-Rouen, Switzerland-Lucerne and around, then back to Paris' in 1866 (Diary, 21 May). The earlier date of the 'Corot' suggests he may have visited there previously, although he could have seen Corot's painting exhibited at the French Gallery. Leader's interest in the French *plein-air* landscapes, and exhibiting his paintings in Paris, was probably instigated by his friend and art dealer, Thomas Wallis, the owner of the French Gallery.

Leader visited the Continent again in 1868, going to France, Germany and Belgium (Diary, 13 May). Although there are no known landscapes by him from these trips, visits to new locations in England during the late 1860s did result in finished paintings. After penning his disillusionment with the Royal Academy in 1867 Leader departed for the Lake District with his sister Patty for a few weeks. He was very pleased with his first visit to the Lakes and hoped to visit them again, which he did the following summer, again with Patty, recording he had 'bought home a lot of work' (6 August, 1868). The fells of Cumbria, like North Wales, had become more accessible to both artist and tourist. It was also a county with a notable literary connection, especially the poetry of Wordsworth which was appended to many a Victorian landscape painting.

The sketches and studies Leader had made on the spot during both trips, and turned into finished works on his return, included scenes of the Lakes Derwentwater, Ullswater and Windermere. A particular favourite was the vale of Keswick along the shores of Derwentwater surrounded by mountains and an inner circle of fells, each having individual characteristics. Among these, featured by Leader, are Walla Crag and Friar's Crag overlooking the eastern shore. An example of his Cumbrian work is a study painted on the spot in 1867 (Colour Plate 18) and a more finished studio painting, dated 1874 (Colour Plate 19). They are of the same scene, namely, Derwentwater from Ladore with Skiddaw in the distance. The only difference in the subject matter is the number of figures, their positions and that of the collie dog. In comparing the style of the two paintings, the latter lacks spontaneity, and is less tangible, because of its high finish. None of Leader's Cumbrian paintings were exhibited at The Royal Academy. Instead, they went to art dealers or were privately commissioned by gentlemen living in Liverpool and Birmingham.

An important Worcestershire landscape which was also not exhibited, although painted at this time, is 'An Autumn Evening on the Severn, near Worcester', 1868 (Colour Plate 20). Initially bought by Thomas Wallis the same year, it was then sold to John Derby Allcroft of Worcester, actual purchase date unknown. Allcroft was one of the successful millionaire

Colour Plate 21. *A Moated Grange. Signed and dated 1868. 28½ x 42in (72.5 x 106.5cm).*
Sefton MBC Leisure Services Department, Arts and Cultural Services Section, The Atkinson Art Gallery, Southport.

entrepreneurs who was in partnership with John Dent, the glove-maker. Together they enjoyed a virtual monopoly as the manufacturers of a product that was in universal use. Allcroft was also MP for Worcester and, in 1889, he purchased and restored the thirteenth century fortified manor house, Stokesay Castle in Shropshire, which he had commissioned Leader to paint in 1876.

The painting of the River Severn, near Worcester is significant both for the subject matter and the method and style employed. It is the first known large pure landscape that Leader had painted of this river which flowed past the family home. Although 'The Chair Mender' (Plate 3, page 19), and 'A Fisherman's Haunt' (Colour Plate 13, page 34), both depict the Severn they are not 'pure' landscapes, whereas in this later painting the subject matter is the River Severn. Both the figures and the trow laden with hay, with its sail lowered, being towed by a horse along the river bank are subordinate to the river scene. Leader, when working on it, mentioned that it was intended to be one of his Royal Academy pictures for that year (Diary, 20 January, 1868). Instead he chose two other Worcester scenes. The first was 'A Fine Morning in Early Spring', No.113, showing Whittington churchyard in which children are depicted gathering primroses with sheep and lambs in the foreground, and the second was 'A Moated Grange', No.128 (Colour Plate 21). This depicts a large gabled and beamed manor house to which access is by a wooden bridge over the moat. Between an ancient leafless and gnarled oak and the house are wide stone steps, leading to the water's edge, on which are seated a figure and dog. According to James Dafforne, writing in *The Art Journal*, both paintings were very well hung, in the main room, on either side of the Royal Academy President's, Sir Francis Grant, principal picture, a portrait of the Earl of Bradford.[24]

There is also a noticeable change of method and style in 'An Autumn Evening on the

Severn' and 'A Moated Grange'. It was mentioned earlier that in 1858 and 1859 Leader had struggled to come to grips with the traditional method of oil painting which entailed rubbing in in brown before applying the coloured glazes. He did not mention attempting it again until 1868 saying only in the interim period that he initially sketched on the canvas in pencil. Both 'A Moated Grange' and 'An Autumn Evening on the Severn' were first rubbed in in brown which is apparent by the tonality of the pictures. Henceforth in his career Leader painted mostly in this traditional method, although applying colours straight on to a light ground would still be reserved for landscapes depicted in bright summer sunlight and those he wished to keep light and delicate, such as the Welsh summer scenes with silver birch trees. *The Art Journal* had noticed the change and did not like it – ' . . . latterly . . . he seems too much inclined to a free use of browns . . . it is not agreeable'.[25] The painting Dafforne was specifically referring to here was 'A Worcestershire Cottage', dated 1870, which was exhibited at the 1870/71 Winter Exhibition at the French Gallery, No.8. Leader's brushwork in these paintings is also more open and fluid with greater attention paid to the overall unity of the composition resulting in a more naturalistic landscape.

Other new, and more naturalistic landscapes emerged from sketching excursions at the end of the 1860s. These included paintings depicting a lock on the River Avon at Stratford with the church of St Nicholas in the background, a result of Leader's visit to Stratford in August 1869. A large painting of this subject, 'Church and Lock at Stratford-on-Avon', was exhibited the following year at the Royal Academy, No.979, whilst a smaller version (Colour Plate 22) was painted for S.C. Hall, the editor/owner of *The Art Journal*. This was engraved, with two others, to illustrate a monograph on Leader for *The Art Journal* series, 'British Artists: Their Style and Character'. In Leader's correspondence with Hall in August and September 1869 concerning the selection of these three paintings we learn that he was 'proud' to be included in the series.[26]

Colour Plate 22.
Church and Lock at Stratford-on-Avon. Signed and dated 1869. 15¼ x 23½in (39 x 59.5cm).
Photograph: Courtesy of Sotheby's.

Pencil sketch 'In Tintern', 1869.

The Art Journal at that time was the most influential periodical with a wide distribution. It was also the only journal which actively and consistently promoted British artists and their work. Leader would have certainly known of this and been aware that such an article on him would bring him to the attention of a wider audience, including potential buyers, than just the exhibition-going London public. We also learn from the letters that the Stratford painting, for engraving, was chosen from photographs which Leader submitted to the journal of the work he had in hand. It was a substitute for another subject, not described, sent earlier in the year to Hall, which he and the publisher Virtue did not think would make a popular engraving. John and George Pike Nicolls (fl. 1841-1887) were the engravers of all three prints and Leader briefly mentioned to Hall that he had touched up and sent the proof of one of the other engraved paintings 'The Church and River at Bettws-y-coed' to Mr Nicolls and that he, Leader, was 'much pleased with its print'. (Letter, 27 September).[27] The third illustration, also a Welsh scene and an upright, was 'The Birch Wood near Capel Curig, North Wales'.

Other new subjects at this time were the romantic ruins of Chepstow Castle and Tintern Abbey in the Wye Valley depicted in moonlight. The former, 'Chepstow Castle', was exhibited at the Royal Academy in 1870, No.167, along with the large Stratford painting mentioned above. Although the whereabouts of 'Chepstow Castle' is now unknown both

Plate 23. *Tintern Abbey - Moonlight on the Wye. Signed and dated 1900. 20 x 30in (51 x 76cm.)*
Photograph: Courtesy of Sotheby's, N.Y.

Colour Plate 28. *Old Mill, Bettws-y-coed. Signed and dated 1875. 19½ x 29½in (49.5 x 75cm).* Courtsey of G.K.N. Photograph: R.Wood.

Colour Plates 28a and 28b. *Old Mill, Bettws-y-coed 1875. Detail of 28.*

carefully balanced composition, however, reveals the artist's skill in his indisputable impressionistic technique. His method of painting ranges from a very thin application of colour through which, in places, the canvas surface can be observed, to thicker, even impasto, overpainting consisting of dashes and dabs of the paintbrush. The combination of these, seemingly, casual brush strokes not only creates an effective and naturalistic scene but also materializes into identifiable details enhancing the viewer's interest. For example, the white highlights, strategically placed, not only act as perspective devices but also resemble the white flower heads of the cow parsley in the foreground, the ducks and their reflections on the water, the washing blowing on the line (note the strings of the apron), the smoke from the chimneys, the sunshine falling on the tree trunks and foliage and the water flowing from the mill. Leader's limited, but equally effective, use of red draws the viewer's eye to the 'Constable' figures and the dog sitting on the river bank and beyond to the items of washing, the woman's skirt and the shaded ridge of the roof. It is without doubt that Leader, in this painting, and others dating from the 1870s, had acquired the facility to imbue his landscapes with natural light in a style uniquely his own.

The month Leader sold the 'Old Mill, Bettws-y-coed' his Diary reveals a third visit had been made to Sir Robert's country estate in Kent during October which was for pleasure – a shooting party (11 December). He had previously attended a shooting party in the autumn of 1872 and said that the Royal Academician 'Millais was one of the party'.[8] There is no mention of Sir Robert after 1875 which is perhaps not surprising as Leader had more important events to note in his Diary.

1876 was a special year for Leader. Whilst Diary entries for January were concerned with

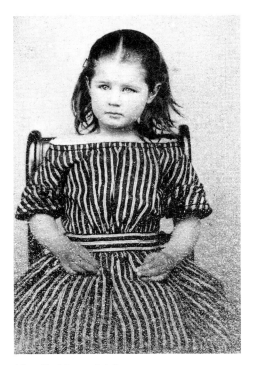

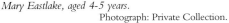

Mary Eastlake, aged 4-5 years.
Photograph: Private Collection.

Mary Eastlake Leader in her mid-20s.
Photograph: Private Collection.

the paintings he was preparing for that year's Royal Academy Exhibition, on 8 February there was, for once, nothing relating to his work. Instead he wrote:

> Today had a letter from one I have advised for years and
> since I have known more of her fondly love she has
> promised to be my wife and now new life dawns upon me.
> God willing that it may add to the happiness of us both.

Although he does not say so, the lady in question was Mary Eastlake (1853-1938), who lived at 'The Brake', Horrabridge, near Plymouth in Devon. Colour Plate 29 (page 52) is a small oil by Leader of the family's dining room). Mary, an artist of flower paintings, was the fourth daughter of William Eastlake, a solicitor and Deputy Judge Advocate of the Fleet.[9] She was also a great niece of Sir Charles Locke Eastlake, President of the Royal Academy from 1850 until his death in 1865. Leader had known Mary since she was a young child from the time when he visited the family home at the invitation of her father for sketching parties. This is where Leader could have first met Sir Robert Collier, as his family home was also at Plymouth.

At first the Eastlake family, especially the eldest son Charles, were against the marriage, presumably because Mary was over twenty years younger than Leader, but more significantly because Leader's family was 'in trade'. The Eastlakes considered themselves to be of the Plymouth gentry. Final acceptance of Leader into the family was probably partly for financial convenience as Mr Eastlake was not a wealthy man and had other daughters, besides Mary, to support. Leader could, and would, give Mary financial security and a very comfortable lifestyle as he had by this time accumulated wealth, not only through his successful career as an artist, but also by shrewdly investing early in companies which were essential to the fast growing industrial economy of Victorian Britain - companies linked to canals, railways, the Post Office, and the Empire's overseas ventures. For Leader, like many successful Victorian entrepreneurs, money could buy one a place in 'society' through marriage. For the impoverished landed gentry such marriages were one of the means to revitalise their own social positions.

Leader's financial position was also, no doubt, one of the factors resulting in the unanimous vote by the Directors of the Worcester Royal Porcelain Company to invite Leader onto the Board in 1876. Leader made no reference to this event which occurred the day after his forty-

Sketching Party.
B.W. Leader second left.
Family Photograph.

fifth birthday, 12 March, when he expressed his disappointment that no letter was received from his future wife. According to the Minutes of the Directors' Meetings, Leader's name does not appear until 11 November, 1878. This could be due to Leader's delayed acceptance because of his forthcoming marriage. He remained a Director for twenty years, during which time he was wealthy enough, in 1885, to lend the Company £8,000 and find £2,000 trust money to enable them to expand.[10] Although he regularly attended the board meetings when living in Worcestershire, his attendance was less frequent after moving to Surrey. The decision to resign in 1898 may have been because of his increased commitment to the Royal Academy and his family which left little time, and perhaps little inclination at the age of sixty-seven years, to travel to Worcester. (According to the Worcester Royal Porcelain Company's records Leader never painted any designs for their ceramics).

Benjamin Williams Leader and Mary Eastlake, who he would always refer to as Fluff, were married on 29 August, 1876 at Buckland Monachorum in Devon; he was forty-five and she was twenty-three. On their wedding day the groom presented the bride with an ormolu travelling case, containing gold-lidded crystal containers and bottles. The honeymoon lasted for three months and Leader tells us they went to Falmouth for two days, Penzance for one

Colour Plate 29. *Interior of*
'The Brake' (Dining room),
Horrabridge, Devon.
14 x 18in (35.5 x 46cm).
Private Collection.
Photograph: R. Cotton.

Colour Plate 30. *St. Michael's Mount. Signed and dated 1877. 17½ x 25½in (44.5 x 64cm).*
Photograph: Courtesy of Phillips.

Colour Plate 32. *An English Hayfield. Signed and dated 1879. 35½ x 54in (90 x 137cm).*
Photograph: R. Cotton. Courtesy of Fine Art of Oakham Ltd.

They built themselves large houses and were a socially cohesive group, which included the Royal Academicians P.H. Calderon (1833-1898), W.Q. Orchardson (1832-1910), G.D. Leslie (1835-1921), H.S. Marks (1829-1898), the Associate G.A. Storey (1834-1919) and D.W. Wynfield (1837-1887). They did not paint any one particular subject but their style was more fluid and naturalistic than the artists who were influenced by the Pre-Raphaelites. Leader felt aggrieved because he believed he had greater claims than MacWhirter, who was younger, but added that he would:

> . . . console myself I am in good company of Cox, Muller,
> Nasmyth, Crome, Linnell, and Dawson[28] . . . , names
> that will live long on after the majority of the present
> R.A.'s and A.R.A'.s are forgotten.[29]

These artists, who Leader mentioned, were landscape painters who had exhibited at the Royal Academy but had never become members. Three days later, on 24 January, 1879, he wrote in his Diary:

> . . . the election as expected – Prinsep,[30] Fildes,[31]
> and MacWhirter. I must plead guilty to being disappointed
> and disheartened for more than 20 years I have exhibited at
> the Academy and have most years held a leading place in
> landscape, and now am no more forward then I was twenty
> years ago – no clique to back me. But I have the
> satisfaction of knowing my pictures are appreciated by the
> public and eagerly sought after – that's more than most of
> the R.A.'s can say at the present.

In a more reflective manner he also wrote that he did not:

> . . . care so much for the honour of being a member but
> I do care that my works should be placed where they can
> be seen, and there is no certainty of that till you are
> made a member.

The Art Journal's comment on the election was diplomatic:

> . . . each has his established right to the distinction,
> though the choice will certainly not pass without
> question; opinion will be divided as to those selected
> and those rejected.

Addressing MacWhirter specifically:

> . . .we beg heartily to congratulate on his election to
> the Associateship.[32]

Leader continued to be bitter about the hanging of his pictures and after he had framed the Swiss scene he was working on for the Royal Academy that year he felt that it was:

> . . . brilliant and effective and cannot fail to advance
> my reputation if it's decently hung by the R.A.'s at the
> Academy: but God help them they are an ignorant lot as
> far as landscape painting - that I am sure of.
> (Diary, 17 February)

Three days later he derived some satisfaction when he learnt that two of his pictures had been sold recently at Birmingham for good prices:

> . . . one, a very early work I sold for £50, brought
> 130gns.; the other, a small but good Thames scene,
> 225gns. . . . I can't help feeling elated at the fact that
> a large and important picture, the one selected by the
> artist (MacWhirter, the new landscape associate of the
> Academy) and his [MacWhirter's] friend Pettie to represent
> him at the Paris Exhibition brought only 42gns. I have the
> public with me if I have not the Academy. So I must
> not grumble.[33]

One reason that Leader's pictures fetched higher prices than those of MacWhirter was probably because Leader was better known in Birmingham as he had been exhibiting there since the early 1850s.

One painting to which Leader devoted a great deal of time in 1879 and which had personal associations for him was 'An English Hayfield', exhibited at the Royal Academy, No.50, (Colour Plate 32, page 57). When working on it he called it 'the Hayfield'. It is a summer scene of a hayfield at Whittington. In the distance the hay is being gathered onto a horse-drawn haywain, whilst in the foreground, amidst the dried hay, are figures which, according to Leader,[34] were posed by his wife, their young son Benjy, and the baby daughter Ethel, who was born in July the previous year. Leader did not record her birth nor would he mention that his wife gave birth to another

An English Hayfield - Detail, mother and children. See Colour Plate 32, page 57.

B.W. Leader's elder brother, Sir Edward Leader Williams, aged 66 years.
Photograph: Private Collection.

B.W. Leader's sister, Maria Patty Williams. Photograph: Private Collection.

B.W. Leader, 1880s.
Photograph: Private Collection.

daughter, christened Beatrice, later that year in November. Three children in the first three years of their marriage! No wonder Leader wrote on 11 February that his wife was 'weak and delicate', but added that 'the children were well'. His father, however, was seriously ill. Leader had been to Diglis House on the evening of 5 February, 'to see my poor father who is sinking fast and will not be long'. On 18 February, Leader and his wife took 'Benjy to see his poor Grandfather who is getting weaker every day and cannot last many days . . . my sister Sarah is there. Dear Father is very quiet and peaceful and thank God without pain'. Mr Edward Leader Williams died on 26 February in his seventy-seventh year.[35] 'My eldest brother [Edward] has been down. We have been very busy making arrangements for the funeral' (27 February). Leader's brother, who had followed his father's profession, was at this time the Engineer of the Bridgewater Navigation Company and living near Manchester.[36]

The Last Will and Testament of Edward Leader Williams senior shows that his estate was valued at under £3,000. After the discharge of his debts and funeral expenses he provided for the maintenance and comfort of his wife, Sarah, and the residue was divided between his ten children. (The eleventh child, Theophilus, had died in 1854, aged fourteen years). No mention is made of Diglis House which suggests that it was probably rented and not owned by the family.

In spite of this very sad year for the family Leader tells us he was financially 'prosperous in his profession . . . Have much to be thankful for as the times are bad for art. I'm one of the few who haven't felt them' (Diary, 11 February). This bad time for Art referred to by Leader was the depression of the art market, especially for modern art, a consequence of the economic depression of the late 1870s.[37] One of the great collectors of Art, Baron Albert Grant, a property promoter, declared bankruptcy and had to sell his vast Art Collection in 1877. This included three 1873 Royal Academy paintings by Leader which the Baron had purchased from Agnew's the year they were exhibited.[38] It was also an especially difficult time for contemporary artists as the 'new' collectors were turning their attention to the old master paintings which had become popular due to the Old Masters' Exhibitions at the Royal Academy during the winter months from the early 1870s.[39] For both the collectors and dealers the old master paintings were seen as sounder investments than those by living artists untested by time.

The depression did not seem to affect Leader. His comment on the Birmingham sale was that his pictures 'made first-rate prices considering the bad times'. His sales records show that his paintings sold during the previous year, 1878, totalled £2,216 for twenty paintings. This included £700 for the large six foot Swiss landscape exhibited at the Royal Academy, No.122, which Leader sold privately to a Mr Crossland. Most of the others were sold to the art dealers, including Arthur Tooth who had a gallery in the Haymarket. Since 1873 Tooth had annually purchased the occasional painting from Leader. But by 1879, when the dealer's Spring Exhibitions were beginning to achieve popularity, he became a more enthusiastic customer of Leader vying for his best works along with Agnew's and Wallis. To ensure he had first choice he took the trouble to visit Leader's studio at Whittington in both 1879 and 1880, and was back again in February 1881. On this last occasion Leader showed him the pictures after dinner by lamp light. The following morning Tooth viewed them again and:

> . . . bought all three for £1,200: also securing three or
> four small pictures. So that is very satisfactory. He
> thinks very highly of the pictures – will exhibit the
> River Scene in his Exhibition. The other two go to
> the Academy.[40]

The River Scene when exhibited at Tooth's 1881 Spring Exhibition was called 'A Welsh Stream in Summertime'. The two for the 1881 Royal Academy Exhibition were a Worcestershire landscape 'February Fill Dyke', No.42, (Colour Plate 33) and a Welsh mountain scene 'Glyder Fawr', No.521. The former Royal Academy painting, 'February Fill Dyke', has become the best known and most popular of all Leader's paintings and is at present on permanent display at the Birmingham City Art Gallery.

In his customary way, Leader was just as meticulous in the preparation of 'February Fill Dyke' as he was with other subjects chosen to be exhibited at the Royal Academy. His working practice was not only to paint various preparatory studies and sketches, but he also, on a number of occasions painted two versions, with minor changes, of the same landscape he wished to exhibit. He then selected, or was advised, which painting to submit to the Royal Academy. In addition, after the painting had been exhibited, and was popular, he would be requested to paint replicas. These were usually smaller versions, either privately commissioned or for engraving by the art dealer who, having originally purchased the Royal Academy exhibit, usually owned the copyright. Unlike many artists, Leader would, if not restrained by the copyright law, sell all his sketches and studies of a particular finished landscape.[41] This is why one can find a number of paintings of the same, or very similar, scenes in various sizes, either on board or canvas, passing through the art market both during Leader's lifetime and still today. As a consequence Leader has been called, and still is, rather unjustly, a repetitious painter. But one has to realize he was a business man, as well as a professional artist, catering to the demand for his work. There is a smaller four foot version of the six foot Royal Academy exhibit of 'February Fill Dyke', also dated 1881, in the Collection of the Manchester City Art Gallery, and an undated two foot version now in a private collection. Leader, himself, recorded in 1881 selling four paintings of this title. As well as purchasing the Royal Academy picture for £400, Tooth also purchased, in August, a smaller version for £220. Another Art dealer, Vokins, bought one for £175 and one was sold to a man called Lea for £300.

The inspiration for 'February Fill Dyke' was recalled by the artist twenty-four years later. He was reported to have said:

> One evening as I looked out of my window at the back
> of the house, I saw the evening sunlight reflected in
> some puddles left by a heavy fall of rain. I had never
> seen that painted before and it occurred to me it would
> not only be new, but it would also make a good subject.
> I therefore decided to paint the picture, which, in part
> at least, represents the view from that window.[42]

Leader only touched briefly on the painting while working on it. He started it in January 1881 and called it a 'November morning' (17 January) becoming, by 13 February, a 'February morning'. At some point after this it became an evening scene. Leader himself subsequently told Lewis Lusk in 1901 that he called the picture 'A November Evening after Rain'.[43]

The final title of the painting was taken from an old country rhyme:

> February fill the dyke
> Be it black or be it white
> But if it be white
> It's the better to like.

The 'white' snow being of greater value to the farmer than the 'black' rain, in this instance the dyke has been filled with the 'black'. The painting marks a pivotal point in Leader's career. It declares how Leader has mastered the effects of light reflected from water. He has exploited, for the first time in 'February Fill Dyke', light reflections in the puddles of rain-filled tracks to illuminate his landscape. Previously he had only employed the traditional subjects to achieve this end – rivers, ponds, and lakes. The combination of his freer brushstrokes, the toning down of the colours, and the attention to the overall unity of the composition, not seen in his previous Royal Academy paintings, greatly enhances the naturalistic effect of the scene. The painting when exhibited at the Royal Academy was extensively reviewed by the art critics who nearly all agreed it was the artist's best picture to date. *The Art Journal* thought the:

> . . . title and picture suit one another well. The
> characteristics of the kind of weather which gives
> the epithet of 'fill dyke' to the month of February
> are most truthfully depicted in the overflowing ponds
> and splashy roads and the pale, streaked evening sky.
> It is a thoroughly English landscape.[44]

The Daily News also commended the truth of ' . . . drawing of the leafless trees and a faintly golden sky in the flooded roads'.[45]

The Graphic, too, praised the picture's '. . . truth and fidelity on the rendering of the individual facts of Nature'.[46] F.G. Stephens of the *Athenaeum* was double-edged in his praise. He thought it was ' . . . more ambitious and stronger, but far less refined and artistic'[47] . . . than a nearby landscape [Twilight in the Comb, No.26] by W.M. Hale (1837-1929). Stephens then went on to say that although he found the '. . . lumination' of Leader's painting 'which is the subject, very happy indeed. The execution is more dexterous than searching, and would bear refining.[48] *The Times* was also double-edged in it appraisal, '. . . the large, fine landscape in Mr. Leader's usual style - very fine in general atmospheric effect and in its rendering of the wet sky and road, but rather poor in its tree drawing and certainly too much varnish.[49] *The Magazine of Art,* after commenting on a landscape by J.G. Naish (1824-1905), disliking what they saw as extreme forms of the Pre-Raphaelite observation - bright colours and excessive detail - turned their attention to Leader who they thought also belonged to the literal school.

Colour Plate 33. *February Fill Dyke.*
Signed and dated 1881.
48 x 72in (122 x 183cm).
Birmingham Museums and Art Gallery.

Of 'February Fill Dyke' they liked the ' . . . real rainy landscape with the quite illusory perspective of the wet road stretching flatly away; all here is fresh in execution and exceeding honest.[50] Leader was well pleased with the response from the critics:

> My 'February Fill Dyke' in the Academy is a success
> and thought to be one of the best landscapes of the
> year. The Academy wished to buy it for the Nation
> with funds from the Chantry Bequest[51] but Tooth
> had already resold it'. (Diary, 9 May)

Tooth had indeed sold it to a John Edward Wilson of Edgbaston, Birmingham. He was a Quaker and founder, with his cousin Albright, of the first British company to produce commercial chemicals - Albright and Wilson. His wife bequeathed the painting to the Birmingham City Art Gallery in 1914.

Tooth was reported by Leader as saying that both the pictures 'February Fill Dyke' and 'Glyder Fawr' ought to ensure his election as an Associate. But Leader tried 'not to think or care the slightest about what the Academy do'.[52] He was fifty, and his first real hope, bordering on expectation, of election, had come sixteen years ago, in 1865. He had been disappointed then and many times since, and he was to be disappointed again on this occasion.

On 19 January, 1882, when he had already begun preparing his Royal Academy pictures for that year, he wrote in his Diary:

> There was an election of two Associates of the Academy
> last night which upset me. I have been told I should be sure
> to come in. Woods [Henry, 1846-1921] and an architect* I
> never heard of was elected.
> (*This was George Frederick Bodley, 1827-1907)

The Art Journal thought Woods was a little-known artist with less ability than some other landscape painters, including Leader. They also believed that landscape painters were very much under-represented among the seventy members (forty-two RAs and twenty-eight ARAs) - there were only six landscapists. It went on to say:

> . . . it is a curious anomaly that whilst, on the one hand,
> these slights are continued to one of the few branches
> of English Art which exhibits distinct vitality, the
> Academy should be proposing to hold an exhibition
> of a deceased 'outsiders' work, Mr. J. Linnell.[53]

John Linnell, whose work Leader admired, had just died (see 'Bid for Fame, Part 1', page 26). Earlier, in 1867, Linnell had declined '. . . the honour proffered for acceptance - admission among the Associates. He is old [74 years] and has achieved fame and fortune without the Royal Academy'.[54] Leader would have had no intention of refusing acceptance as an Associate if he were elected. In retrospect one can only speculate why the Royal Academy delayed Leader's election. If age was a criterion then he did have a stronger claim over the younger landscape painters Peter Graham, elected 1877, and John MacWhirter elected in 1879. He had also exhibited at the Royal Academy's Exhibitions for longer than either artist. In addition, by the end of the 1870s, Leader had become one of the most popular living landscape artists with the general public. His paintings were in greater demand than those of his friend George Vicat Cole even though Cole had become a full member of the Royal Academy in 1880.

The critics acknowledged Leader's popularity although the general consensus was that his work was popular because it was 'facile' and 'literal'. These were qualities which, the critics believed, made a painter popular but not an intellectual artist. It was also the consensus that those of discerning taste demanded more of a landscape - imagination, sentiment, mood. Whilst this view would have been carried by the Royal Academy's Council, who were dominated by the St John's Wood clique, it still does not fully explain why the Royal

Plate 34. *'In the evening it shall be light'.** Signed and dated 1882. 46 x 80in (117 x 203cm).* Photograph: *Art Annual,* Supplement of 'Art Journal', 1901, page 1.

Academy continually chose to bypass Leader. Perhaps jealousy was the motive because of the popularity of his landscapes with the public.

On 12 May, 1882 Leader's three pictures for that year's Royal Academy exhibition were almost finished and, as he wrote in his Diary, ' . . . had been seen by a great number of friends and thought my best. I only hope the R.A. think so too'. The favourite was what Leader called the 'evening church yard scene' when working on it (Plate 34). Some years later, in 1901, when he was interviewed by *The Strand Magazine* for their series 'Paintings Preferred by their Painters', Leader said this favourite painting was a scene of Whittington and its old church.[55] He was also reported to have said that he remembered when speaking of making an important picture of the scene his wife was strongly against it:

> She said that a churchyard in winter-time would
> make such a dismal subject and she held to this opinion
> all the time that I was making my sketches. But somehow
> or other I always had a strong faith in the subject
> and painting it was a labour of love.[56]

The title of the painting occurred, according to Leader,[57] when the Dean of Worcester, Lord Alywne Compton and his wife, were on a visit to the artist at his home. On looking at the picture, Lady Compton immediately quoted the biblical words 'at evening time it shall be light'[58] as being a particularly apt title for the scene. Impressed with the suggestion Leader adopted it, although when the painting was exhibited at the Royal Academy, No.737, it was called 'In the evening there shall be light'.

The church in the painting has proved problematic. It is supposed to be a likeness of the old fourteenth/fifteenth century church, whose churchyard bordered onto the land of Whittington Lodge. The church was demolished in 1842, twenty years before Leader took up residence in the village. Although Leader said he had painted this church 'with assistance of a pencil sketch lent to him by a friend in the neighbourhood', the church in his painting is unlike the two pencil drawings in existence. One is dated 1784, and the other was sketched just before the old church was demolished. The drawings depict a half-timbered building with tiled roof over the nave and chancel and very little in the way of windows which were square. In Leader's painting the building is stone with more windows which seem to be pairs of lights with trefoiled heads. At the west (nave) end of the roof of the old church was a squat timber-slatted bell turret. This is replaced in the painting by a single stone belfry. The porches in both are similar, but Leader has placed his on the north side whereas in the drawings of the old church it is on the south. The new church, consecrated on 19 March, 1844, is very different from either the drawings or Leader's painting, having lancet windows and a distinctive tall bell turret. The church in the painting is a mystery. Is it a composite church or does the original still stand somewhere in Worcestershire? Perhaps it does not matter, although Leader did paint a number of other churches which can be positively identified. It is possible that the artist deliberately placed the porch on the north side, to lead one's eye from the path, through the gate to the porch and because he wanted to silhouette the landscape against the evening sky in the west. The great yew tree depicted in the painting still stands in the church yard at Whittington north of the church. There are also in existence three pencil sketches and a pen

* Note how the title of this painting has changed since first exhibited. (Plates 34a and 34b)

Colour Plate 34a. *'At evening time it shall be light'. Signed and dated 1897. 30 x 50in (76.5 x 127cm).*
Manchester City Art Galleries.

Colour Plate 34b. *'In the evening there shall be light'.*   Photograph: Courtesy of Maas Gallery, London.

and ink drawing by Leader, all unsigned and not dated, which are supposed to be of old Whittington church but these have to be disputed.

'In the evening there shall be light' was purchased by Agnew's in March 1882 for £500 and immediately resold to Sir John Pender of Atlantic Cable fame. All the critics who reviewed the painting at the Royal Academy were, with the exception of one, unanimous in their praise for the painting; 'coarsely painted' was the terse comment of *The Art Journal*. Subsequently, *The Art Journal* changed its mind, presumably because of the success of the picture and Leader's election into the Royal Academy. In 1901 Lewis Lusk waxed lyrical:

> . . . we are all agreed that 'In the evening it shall
> be light' [note change of title] is his finest production, most simple and
> strong in technique, most poetically suggestive
> in meaning.[59]

Lusk seemed to mean that there was an allegory between the painting's old church, its black yew trees, and mossed tombstones, with the experience of what a human has to endure during his life - having endured a heavy day of storm, the evening sun casts its light over the land foretelling hope of a fine tomorrow. There is, however, no suggestion in the Diary that Leader consciously attributed allegorical meaning to this landscape, although a proverbial biblical quotation was given for the title.

Lusk mentioned the tombstones in the churchyard and the illustration of the Royal Academy painting in the 1901 *Art Annual* depicts them. They are also depicted in a later, but smaller version, of the Royal Academy painting, dated 1897, which is in the collection of the Manchester City Art Gallery (Colour Plate 34a). But today the tombstones are no longer visible in the Royal Academy painting (Colour Plate 34b), having been edited out at some time between 1923 and 1958, possibly at the request of a purchaser. (The tombstones had also been overpainted, this century, but now recently restored, in the large study of the Royal Academy painting. This, too, was purchased by Agnew's for £400 who immediately resold it for £787.10s to Samuel Armitage the textile manufacturer).

Tombstones, like skulls, predicting mortality were for some people especially unwelcome details in paintings. The over-brillant colour on the unbroken horizon line between the yew tree and the church (Colour Plate 34b), which was originally broken by tombstones (Plate 34, and Colour Plate 34a), now creates an unbalanced composition. It it inconceivable that the artist, during his lifetime would have made such an alteration, or sanctioned it to be done by others even though he did not own the copyright. He was extremely proud of the painting which brought him honour when exhibited in Paris in 1889 (see 'Recognition and Success, Part 2', pages 77 and 78). Whilst Leader would not have altered this painting he has been known to alter another, less important work on request. An art dealer recounts a story about his father-in-law (who was also a dealer) writing to Leader to request the removal of tombstones from one of his paintings as it was not selling. Leader replied in person by arriving at the Gallery and agreed to alter it.

In addition to 'In the evening there shall be light', Leader did not know which of his other two pictures to send to the Royal Academy as his second exhibit. The choice was between the morning river scene which he titled 'Banks of the Ivy O', a composite scene of Bredon Church by the River Avon, or the cottages and wet road after a storm picture titled 'Stonehall Common, Worcestershire'. The former was finally decided upon because it offered a 'greater contrast to the church evening picture'. It was retitled 'Morning: the Banks of the Ivy O!', No.550. When selecting his pictures for the Royal Academy Leader was always concerned not to submit similar scenes. They were always different in either effect or in the location of the landscape so that they could be judged on their own merits.

'In the evening there shall be light' and the previous year's Royal Academy painting 'February Fill Dyke', two Worcestershire winter scenes and the 'wettest' ever exhibited at the Royal Academy, finally achieved for Leader what he had long worked hard for - election as an Associate of the Royal Academy, on 16 January, 1883.

Colour Plate 35. *Self-Portrait. Signed and dated 1884. 13½ x 11¾in (34.5 x 30cm).* City of Aberdeen Gallery and Museums Collections.

Recognition and Success (Part 1)
1883-1888

Last night I was elected an associate of the Royal Academy I heard I had a good chance but tried not to think about it but go on with my work quietly. I was woken at quarter past eleven by telegram from Brett informing me I was elected by a large majority. Brock,[1] another Worcester man, and Holls[2] the engraver came in with me . . . (Diary, 17 January, 1883)

There is a sense of calm satisfaction in these words, but Leader must surely have felt deeply gratified that he had finally succeeded in attaining associate membership after exhibiting sixty paintings at the Royal Academy's Summer Exhibitions during the previous twenty-nine years.

To be elected an Associate did not mean an artist would automatically become a full member after a certain time. To become a full member involved another electoral procedure, and for Leader it would be fifteen years before he was elected into the 'inner sanctum'. After the official notification Leader had to proceed with the obligatory rituals for a newly elected member. In February 1883 he went twice to London, first to receive his Diploma and then to

Self-portrait, B.W.L., aged nineteen. Signed 'Benjy Williams 1850'. Board. Private Collection.

dine at the Royal Academy Club and make courtesy calls on all the Royal Academicians which he said was 'hard work . . . did not manage more than 25 or 30'[3] (Diary, 19 February). He was also fêted in his home town, Worcester, with a dinner held in his honour by his friends and members of the Union Club.[4]

As a consequence of these additional social commitments, Leader's account of his work that year was brief. He was already well advanced with his six main pictures (river scenes of the Llugwy, Thames, Severn, Avon, Teme and Salwarpe) so it was just a matter of finishing them and selecting two or three for the Royal Academy. By the middle of March Leader had sent Tooth his largest river scene, 'The Valley of the Llugwy', which was exhibited at that dealer's Spring Exhibition, No.59. The painting was purchased by Henry Tate, head of the Sugar Refineries in Liverpool and London, and later included in his art collection which was donated to the nation.[5] That same year, unlike Tooth, Morland Agnew and Vokins visited Leader's studio at Whittington. Agnew purchased two of the intended Royal Academy exhibits, 'Parting Day' and 'Green Pastures and Still Waters' which were resold to Sir William Cuthbert Quilter, one of the founders of the National Telephone Company. The third Royal Academy painting that year, 'An Autumn Evening' was sold to Vokins. Unfortunately, it is not known in which private collection this river scene was placed.

A painting not recorded by Leader, but mentioned by Lusk in 1901, is a self-portrait requested by Alexander MacDonald Jnr. from Perthshire, whose father had amassed his fortune in the granite industry. MacDonald collected self-portraits from artists who had just become Royal Academy members and Leader duly obliged with his own (Colour Plate 35). This is the only known authenticated self-portrait by Leader although another does exist. Signed 'Benjy Williams 1850' on the reverse, it is, according to the family, supposed to have been painted when he was about nineteen years old (above). Whilst there are similar facial features, especially in the eyes and nose, to those in two photographs of Leader taken aged

B.W. Leader, aged nineteen.
Photograph. *The Strand Magazine*,
June 1892, p.599.

B.W. Leader, aged 25-26 years?
Photograph: Private Collection.

nineteen years and when he was about twenty-five (left), the earlier portrait would appear to be of a lad younger then nineteen. There is another photograph, or rather a photo-montage, of Leader, as a private in an unidentified Volunteer Unit taken about the mid-1850s (opposite). Although this is a studio posed photograph of Benjamin, on the left, and his companion which has been superimposed on another photograph identified as the gateway of the Edgar Tower at Worcester Cathedral, it has not been possible to state whether it was a Worcester or London Unit.[6]

Leader clearly received many commissions following his election in 1883 because he wrote in the following January, 'I am behind with my Academy pictures this year having been kept hard at work by the dealers painting too many pictures but it was inevitable' (Diary, 27 January, 1884). The other dealers requesting paintings included Wallis and McLean; the latter, like Tooth, had a Gallery in the Haymarket, No.7, at which he too held exhibitions, but of smaller oils and watercolours.

Leader's total sales figures for 1883 of thirty-three paintings, including studies and sketches, was £7,300. Never again would his annual income from his paintings be so high. Although his total annual output had not altered since the 1870s the prices he could now command for his pictures as an Associate Royal Academician were higher. For example, paintings between six and eight feet were now selling for £500 - £800, a rise of approximately £100 per foot since the 1870s. The irony of such prices was that the figures depicted in many of his landscapes, the agricultural workers who dwelt in the 'picturesque' thatched cottages, and tended the livestock and harvested the fields, would have been taking home an average wage of only £35 per annum,[7] a sum which Leader could earn with a small 8in x 12in sketch painted in less than a single day.

The highest price Leader ever received was for a landscape painted in 1886. A long standing patron and friend, Charles Lea of Worcester paid £1,000 for a Welsh mountain landscape 'With Verdure Clad' (Colour Plate 36, page 71). It was Leader's largest painting to date, an eight foot canvas, and said by him to be his most 'ambitious picture' (23 January, 1886). Recent research has pin-pointed the location of this summer scene. It was painted near Capel Curig and the buildings in the middle distance are those of Bryn Bethynau farm above the main A5 road almost opposite Cyfyng Falls. The stream in the foreground would flow down to meet the River Llugwy in the valley below although only its wooded slopes are depicted. Above the distant ridge looms the mountain Moel Siabod.

Leader had first offered the painting to Morland Agnew and Arthur Tooth but they declined to buy it because, according to Leader, the price was too high and the size made it unsaleable (Diary, 8 March, 1886), factors which were not commensurate with a depressed contemporary art market. Leader confirmed the lack of interest in current art later in the month after he had returned from London, where he had seen one of his other smaller 1886 Royal Academy exhibits, a Worcestershire cottage scene 'The End of the Day', hanging in Agnew's gallery. He recalled that Agnew's was only buying very few pictures for the Royal Academy '. . . only Peter Graham, one of mine and . . . [one] . . . by Vicat Cole. I was glad to get away from Town there is little doing in the art world and the artists are depressed' (Diary, 26 March). Landscapes by Graham, Leader, and Cole were the most popular with collectors and Agnew's, no doubt, relied on that continued popularity, while ignoring the growing criticism by a number of major art critics who believed these artists were just catering to public demand. 'With Verdure Clad' was exhibited at the Royal Academy, No.964, and Leader recalled with great satisfaction that it was, along with his two other exhibits (the cottage scene mentioned above and a Welsh mountain lake scene), very popular despite the harsh comments

B.W. Leader (left) with companion in volunteer army uniform. Photomontage.
Private Collection.

by many of the critics. Frederick G. Stephens, writing in *The Athenaeum*, thought the painting
'painty and fallacious'.[8] The critic also had harsh words to say about Leader's other paintings
and concluded that:

> . . . The easy-going sentimentalities of Mr Leader,
> Mr. V. Cole, and Mr. P. Graham are welcome only where
> nature is little studied. But the popularity of their
> pictures will not survive that growth of knowledge
> and taste which will consign to oblivion the flashy
> landscapes of the last decade.[9]

The Times critic preferred the quieter and less ambitious 'The End of the Day', because of
the '. . . care of drawing of the trees . . . and . . . the abstinence from the use of hot yellows', a
criticism he had often made of Leader's paintings since the early '80s. His only comment of
'With Verdure Clad' was that it was the principal painting in one of the larger rooms.[10] Leader
thought the criticisms were unjust because his ' . . . works were never more popular. I gained
the first and second largest number of votes in the *Pall Mall Gazette* . . . [?] . . . for the best
landscape. My large Welsh picture "With Verdure Clad" being first and "The End of the
Day" second' (Diary, January 1887).
    The votes mentioned by Leader were the result of a competition-cum-survey organised by

B.W. Leader's daughters: Ethel, Mary and Beatrice.
Photograph: Private Collection.

*B.W. Leader's sons: Benjamin
Eastlake and his younger
brother Edward.*
Photograph: Private Collection.

The Pall Mall Gazette on 4 May, 1886 (see Appendix 1). The aim of the survey was to allow the 'popular voice' instead of the 'artistic coteries' to articulate on the merits of the pictures in that year's Summer Exhibition. The results were published on Monday, 16 August, based on nearly two thousand votes from throughout Britain and overseas. From the results of the poll (see Appendix 2) for 'The Best Landscape' the two paintings mentioned by Leader received the highest number of votes. They beat those by his fellow friends and artists, Cole and Davies, who were by then Royal Academicians. Even Leader's Welsh mountain lake scene, No.346, which was twelfth out of twenty-three paintings came out ahead of the landscape by Peter Graham, also a Royal Academician.

Although Leader was continuing to paint and exhibit Welsh landscapes, they were not being produced in such great numbers as they had been in the '60s and '70s. Those of the 1880s are, with a few exceptions, variations of earlier works or drawn from his existing supply of sketches, the River Llugwy being a favourite feature. One original subject, though, is 'The Old Holyhead Road', 1885, painted from where the road went over the Cyfyng bridge just below Capel Curig. The mood of the scene is sombre with clouds half veiling the mountains and the Llugwy swollen by a storm to become a raging torrent. The painting, when exhibited at the Royal Academy in 1885, No.1033, did not receive good reviews. *The Times* critic held back no punches when he wrote that it was:

> . . . thin . . . artificial . . . conventional in detail, the
> colour passes by crude transitions from yellow lights
> to black shadows; and a study of the picture leads one
> to meditate once more on that secret of popularity in
> art . .˙. Mr Leader seems to paint Nature because it occurs
> to him that he can make a picture out of her . . . others
> paint her either because they love her . . . or because
> they wish to capture her variety of moods . . .'[11]

The Art Journal thought the painting lacked imagination but later, in 1901, Lusk – by then the *Journal's* editor – thought it was a '*chef d'oeuvre* of tremendous power, which ought to be the property of the nation'.[12]

From 1888 Leader introduced a new Welsh subject – coastal scenes of the sandy bays of Cardiganshire and Carnarvonshire. The first such painting to be exhibited was 'The Sands of Aberdovey', No.421, at the 1888 Royal Academy Exhibition. The painting was the result of oil sketches (Colour Plate 37) made during a 'working' holiday with his family at Towyn, near Aberdovey, during the early autumn of 1887. The family had now grown to five children. The two youngest were Mary Elizabeth, born 1880, and Edward Eastlake, born 1882. Towyn would not have been an unusual choice for a family

Colour Plate 36. *With Verdure Clad. Signed and dated 1886. 42 x 87in (106.5 x 221cm).*
Reproduced by permission of Worcester City Museum and Art Gallery.

Colour Plate 37. *The Sands of Aberdovey. Signed and dated 1888. 10 x 14in (25.5 x 35.5cm).*
Photograph: Courtesy of Richard Green, London.

vacation as the Cardigan Bay coast was fast becoming a favourite resort for Victorians. This was especially so for those living in the Midlands whence there was direct rail access by way of Dovey Junction. Indeed, the Welsh coast remains popular with Midlanders to this day and a direct train service still plies between Birmingham and Aberystwyth.

Leader was a little apprehensive when first working on his six foot coastal landscape in the winter of 1887/8. He thought it 'rather weak for so large a picture' (5 January, 1888), but as he continued to paint he felt more confident, saying it was 'very delicate full of light' (11 January). Later in the year, after the Royal Academy Exhibition, Leader wrote that his coast scene, like his other exhibits, was very popular, but ignored by the critics.[13] However, one critic, F.G. Stephens of *The Athenaeum*, briefly commented that although it was 'a better subject' and 'finer and prettier' than 'An Old English Homestead', No.408, which he thought was 'painty' and 'thoroughly mannered',[14] it still demanded the same criticism.

The subjects which dominated Leader's output in the 1880s, far more than his Welsh landscapes, were those of the Worcestershire countryside. During the previous two decades, probably not wishing to be classed as a provincial artist, he had looked beyond his home county for landscape subjects. However, in the 1880s he gathered his material from the flatter countryside of Worcestershire to produce some of his finest paintings. Like John Constable before him, Leader painted best what he knew best and this was, for Leader, Worcestershire's rivers, its leafy lanes, commons and fields, and its villages and churches. Although depicted at different times of the year, the scenes are usually bathed in an amber glow of the setting sun or the harsher brightness of early morning after rain. It would be easy for those who have not experienced the vast expanse of the Worcestershire skies, which fill half of Leader's canvases, at these particular times of day to dismiss his use of bright colours, red, orange, and yellow, as unnatural. It would also be wrong, as it had been with the nineteenth century London art critics viewing such painted skies, to condemn Leader's truth to nature as artificial and contrived. Good examples of his Worcestershire skies in the morning and evening after rain are, 'At evening time it shall be light', 1882 (Colour Plate 34a, page 64) which is thought to be located at Whittington and 'Worcestershire, Morning clearing up after Rain', 1887 (Colour Plate 38, page 74) probably a village in the Vale of Evesham. Another landscape, 'A Worcestershire Lane after a summer shower' of 1885 (Colour Plate 39, page 75), a delightful Crome-like subject, depicts trees and hedgerows washed by a summer shower in a rather more light and delicate manner than was customary in Leader's work at that time.

It may be no coincidence that Leader's first paintings to be etched, printed and sold commercially by his London dealers were Worcestershire scenes. His popularity by this time had reached an audience beyond the exhibition-going public and the wealthy art collectors and for those who were unable to afford Leader's paintings, etched prints of them now offered a cheaper alternative. A few landscapes by Leader had been engraved previously in the 1870s by John and George Pike Nicolls, Edward Cousen (1813?-1889) and Arthur Willmore (1814-1888), but these had been commissioned by the proprietors of *The Art Journal* to illustrate their magazine.[15] It was only from the 1880s that the extent of Leader's popularity is demonstrated by the number of his Royal Academy paintings etched and sold commercially through the art market (see Appendix 5 for engravings/ etchings produced after paintings by Leader). 'February Fill Dyke' was the first Royal Academy painting to be etched by Thomas N. Chauvel (1831-1909), one of the many French etchers who came over to London to escape the Paris Commune and tended to take over the work of the English engravers. The print, 17¼in x 23⅝in, was published in

London and Paris on 1 June, 1884, in an edition including 300 Artist's proofs. It was also published in America where the copyright was registered in Washington. Tooth also had the 1882 Royal Academy painting 'Morning, Banks on the Ivy O' etched by T.N. Chauvel and it was advertised by the art dealer in the catalogue for his 1884 Winter Exhibition. He offered 'Artist's proofs on Vellum, 8gns.; Artist's proofs on Japanese paper, 2gns.; and prints, 1gn.'

Agnew's had Leader's other 1882 Royal Academy painting 'In the evening there shall be light' etched by another Frenchman, Brunet-Debaines in 1886. The announcement of the print, entitled 'At Evening Time', had national, and international coverage, in *The Times*. The author of the piece added his own comments on the superior technical skill of the etcher over that of Leader as a painter saying:

> Of Mr Leader as a painter, in the technical sense of the term we have not the very highest opinion; but there can be no doubt whatever that his pictures etch well. They are generally composed with much skill, their light and shade is very effectively distributed, and they touch a chord of feeling which is common to all. Hence the success of Chauvel's pair of etchings; and hence will come the success of this plate of M. Brunet-DeBaines. He has certainly done all that an etcher can do with such a subject and his work is sure to be very popular.[16]

DeBaines' etchings of the artist's landscapes were popular with the public, but this was mainly due to the success of Leader's paintings in their original oil medium and his working method. From the 1880s Leader's favoured method was to initially paint his canvas in monochrome from sketches and studies of a chosen scene.

Etching of 'February Fill Dyke' by T. Chauvel, 1884 after the 1881 painting by B.W. Leader. Victoria & Albert Picture Library.

In an interview he is quoted as saying he believed in the power of black and white:

> If a picture did not look well in black and white it would
> never turn out as it should in colours. Light and shade are
> literally everything in landscape art.[17]

Examples of his organization of dark masses silhouetted against a lighter background can be seen in paintings such as 'February Fill Dyke' and 'In the evening there shall be light'. Although the etchings were of his Royal Academy paintings, it is evident from his sales records that it was Leader's practice to paint smaller replicas specifically for etching. For example, in June 1886 Leader wrote '"Parting Day", small replica for etching, Agnew's, £100'.[18] The larger painting of the same title and subject had been exhibited at the Royal Academy in 1883, No.98.

One Worcestershire scene was an important commission for Leader because it was '. . . a presentation picture to the Bishop of Ely; a view from the deanery drawing room window of the River Severn and Malvern hills. A subscription for £500 is being made for the purpose' (Diary, 27 January, 1886). The painting originally entitled 'The River Severn from the Deanery', now called 'Smooth Severn Stream', (Colour Plate 40) was presented to Lord Alwyne Compton at Worcester Guildhall in November 1886 in honour of his appointment as Bishop of Ely and for his six years of service as Dean of Worcester Cathedral. The scene is literal, almost topographical, in so much as every object would have been recognisable to those familiar with Worcester at that time. In the middle of the picture the River Severn, under an almost cloudless summer sky, flows past

Colour Plate 38. *Worcestershire: Morning clearing up after Rain. Signed and dated 1887. 17 x 29¾in (43.5 x 75.5cm).*
Reproduced by permission of Worcester City Museum and Art Gallery.

Colour Plate 41. *The Silent Evening Hour. Signed and dated 1890. 56½ x 84in (143.5 x 213cm).* Photograph: Courtesy of Christie's.

By November 1889 the family had settled into Burrows Cross House. According to Leader they had travelled down in their carriage from Malvern on 7 August arriving at the new home during the middle of the day (The carriage referred to must have been a railway carriage otherwise they would not have arrived the same day). Not everyone, it seems, was happy to move house, ' . . . the children scampering over the house and garden very excited and I think very pleased with everything not so the domestics, almost all of them have been a worry and a trouble to us during our move'.[13] Although the neighbours had been very welcoming, Leader did feel it rather a 'task' having to return all the calls but was compensated by 'getting to know the country and enjoyed some splendid drives'.[14] He also mentioned they were all in good health except for his eldest son, Benjamin, who was recovering at home from a bad leg injury sustained while playing football at his boarding school in Malvern.[15]

One of the paintings Leader chose to exhibit at the Royal Academy in 1890 was of Burrows Cross House amidst the fir trees on the heathland (Colour Plate 41). Much of the picture was completed outdoors in front of his subject in a portable iron studio which he had purchased from the amateur artist, Sir Arthur Clay.[16] This painting was the first of many painted in the grounds of his property and a great number of these would feature the clump of fir trees to the west of the house. The style is much looser, almost impressionistic, especially in the foreground detail, than any of his previous Royal Academy pictures. This is partly explained by the trouble it caused Leader when he was working on it. Unable to obtain a balanced composition he said he 'scraped out the greater part of the foreground . . . and painted it again also altering the house making it better in form'.[17] He was also concerned because he thought the subject was not 'sufficiently interesting for so large a canvas and would not sell'.[18] Leader need not have worried because Morland Agnew purchased it for £800. Exhibited as 'The Silent Evening Hour' No.672, the painting attracted less attention from the critics than his two other smaller exhibits, Welsh coastal landscapes 'The Sandy Margins of the Sea', No.131, and 'Where Sea and River Meet', No.458, although it did receive publicity by being illustrated in *The Art Journal*.[19] Leader also had difficulties when working on 'The Sandy Margins of the Sea', not because he could not get it right, but because he had been 'driven wild with interruptions every time I begun to work that I was obliged to put it away'.[20] Work time for

Leader was sacred. He worked on his paintings all morning until lunchtime and for an hour, sometimes longer, in the afternoon. No interruptions from outside were permitted during these hours - even from the family.

During the winter of that year Leader had his second exhibition at the French Gallery. It was in effect a retrospective exhibition because the majority of the forty-three works displayed spanned his career from the 1850s to the present time. Exhibits included a number of Royal Academy paintings lent by their owners. The earliest of these, 'The Young Mother' (Colour Plate 4) exhibited in 1856, was still owned by Leader and the latest exhibit 'The Sandy Margins of the Sea' was in the possession of a Rev. S. Cheshire. Other paintings included finished studies and replicas of early Royal Academy works. To Leader's surprise the review notices in the Press were more favourable than he expected 'even my old enemies . . . and the worst any of them can do is to sneer at my popularity'.[21] *The Saturday Review* had the most favourable article, writing that:

> . . . The French Gallery has formed a delightful selection
> from the works of this popular artist. The striking aspects
> of nature that Mr Leader selects are made more emphatic
> by his bold handling of his subjects, his execution skill is
> more real than his vapid critics are wont to acknowledge.
> Here are displayed the quieter as well as the more angry
> moods of nature . . .[22]

The reviewer concluded with an assessment of a few individual pictures. *The Times* critic was one of the 'sneerers'. His early advice to Leader had been not to have an exhibition of his paintings because people would discover at once how much of his art was done on a system and how little of exact observation of nature went into the making of his pictures.[23] But now the critic forecasted that the exhibition was sure to be a success because Leader's work was 'popular and facile'. Moreover, it would be a greater success, according to the critic, than a previous exhibition of works by a much more distinguished artist, the German Von Uhde,[24] held at the French Gallery, which had been a financial failure.[25]

Although *The Illustrated London News* thought it was a misuse of nearly half the wall space to devote it to the pictures of so essentially an English artist as Leader who, even though honoured by the French nation, had made 'not a single concession to the French School of Painting', the journal concluded that the artist's work:

> . . . clean and conscientious is thoroughly English
> growing out of the tradition of a school which modelled
> itself upon Dutch Masters, like Hobbema, Cupy and others.
> It is sometimes hard in outline, more often crude in colour,
> but it is always completely thorough . . . How he succeeded
> his career amply testifies, for he occupies at the present
> time a foremost and almost unchallenged position as a
> painter of pure landscapes.[26]

Stephens of *The Athenaeum* described the collection as 'machine-made', singling out 'The Sandy Margins of the Sea' for special attention:

> A noteworthy example of the extreme cleverness and
> half-sincerity of the painter, who is content with
> appealing to the popular taste by studies of nature
> dextrous rather than sound quasi-poetic effects; the
> sentiments of which even the dullest observer cannot
> miss.[27]

Stephens had a habit of pencilling comments in his Exhibition catalogues next to titles of paintings. In his French Gallery catalogue there was 'beastly' against 'The Sandy Margins of the Sea', and 'too cold' next to the 1883 Royal Academy painting 'Green Pastures and Still Waters'. Leader fared better in *The Daily News* who thought the collection comprised his finest works:

> His easily-intelligible style has created for him a
> large popularity, which the present exhibition will
> certainly increase . . . The variety is great but it is in
> the subject rather than the treatment . . . His
> interpretation of Nature does not attempt to render
> her subtleties or to discover and reveal her secrets.
> He paints what he sees (as the Impressionist school boast
> that they do), but he sees what is plain to all. And hence
> his great and growing popularity.[28]

Leader was still not too old to produce new subjects. In 1891, at the age of sixty, he exhibited at the Royal Academy his first and only industrial subject 'The Manchester Ship Canal: Works in Progress at Eastham, Sept 1890', No.590 (Colour Plate 42), which had been commissioned by Lord Egerton, the Chairman of the Canal Company. The commission is explained by the fact that Leader's eldest brother, Edward Leader Williams, was the canal's chief engineer and in charge of its construction.[29] It was necessary for Leader to visit the site in Lancashire twice to make preparatory sketches and 'wretched weather' had to be endured during both trips. On one of the visits Leader overheard one workman telling another, standing nearby watching him work, 'that bloke [Leader] has a fist which won't let him

Colour Plate 42. *The Manchester Ship Canal: Works in Progress at Eastham, Sept. 1890. Signed and dated 1891. 53¾ x 88in (136.5 x 223.5cm).*
The National Trust Photo Library.

The Studio, Burrows Cross House. Photograph: Courtesy of Frost & Reed, London.

starve.[30] How right they were! At the end of the following year Leader was to write that his income from his earnings 'would be more than enough for many, but we don't lack for nothing, large house, eight servants, governess, Benjy at school etc., etc., etc.'.[31]

Leader's treatment of one of Britain's major nineteenth century engineering feats was similar in style to his countryside scenes. The viewer is never made aware of the hard work, or the poverty, of the country 'folk' in a Leader landscape because the figures are small, unobtrusive and wander along village tracks to and from work in the cold light of the morning or under the glow of the evening sun. They stroll or sit in churchyards on balmy summer afternoons, fish or picnic by peaceful rivers or just populate views of beauty spots. Even figures tending the cattle or sheep are resting and his hay-makers and wood-gatherers hardly seem to bend in their work. In 'The Manchester Ship Canal: Works in Progress at Eastham, Sept. 1890', the viewer is not expected to be concerned with the arduous labour of the men, working like ants, at the base of the lock. Instead, the beholder is invited to admire from afar the enormous undertaking of such a construction.

Leader painted two large pictures of the project, a six foot and the other over seven foot, for Lord Egerton to choose from. On a visit to Burrows Cross House he selected the larger. It seems that Leader had no option but to allow Lord Egerton to have the picture at the price agreed earlier, £600, which was really the cost for the smaller size because he had painted two versions without consulting his client. The artist was a little put out because he wrote, 'I should like him to know I have for years got £800 from the Trade for that size [seven foot] picture'.[32] Lord Egerton gave his permission for Leader to sell the smaller version, which was purchased by Agnew's who had already admired it. When Egerton's painting was exhibited at the Royal Academy it received the briefest of reviews from only a small number of critics in spite of Leader's claim that it was 'a great success'. *The Art Journal* found it 'finely designed but metallic'[33] and *The Times* thought it was 'an interesting attempt to give pictorial value to the

works of the Manchester Ship Canal'.[34] Leader recorded his disappointment that the painting did not make him a Royal Academician in an election held in 1891.

Ten days before Christmas Leader wrote that the weather had been bad during the summer and autumn of 1891. Being an artist who had to paint his preliminary sketches and studies outside in front of his chosen subjects meant he was behind with his Royal Academy pictures for the following year. It was a situation which could not be remedied until after the New Year because there was to be a children's dance at the house and Helen, Leader's unmarried sister, and the Scottish landscape artist, David Murray, 1849-1933,[35] would be staying over Christmas.[36] The dances, held in Leader's large studio, soon became a regular Christmas event at Burrows Cross House and one of the main social events of the season in the neighbourhood until the First World War. The studio was one of the additions to the house designed by Norman Shaw for Leader. It was two storeys high with the roof curving up as in a medieval manorial hall. Along one wall there was a flight of stairs to a minstrels' gallery, from where the band would play during the dances.

Whilst the grounds surrounding the house provided Leader with an abundance of artistic subjects, he also found much to interest him in the nearby villages. The twelfth century church of St James in Shere, the family's local parish church, was the subject for a finished

Pencil sketch of Shere church. This church is shown on the easel in the picture below.

B.W. Leader in his Studio, Burrows Cross House.
Photograph: *Art Annual* 1901, supplement of 'Art Journal', page 25.

Colour Plate 43. *Shere Church. Signed and dated 1892. 30 x 48in (76 x 122cm).*   Manchester City Art Galleries.

Plate 44. *An Old Country Churchyard 'With ivy mantle clad'. Signed and dated 1893. 48 x 72in (122 x 183cm).* Photograph: 'Royal Academy Pictures 1893'.

work painted in 1892 (Colour Plate 43) and sold to John E. Yates, the largest cotton spinner in Rochdale. In this morning summer scene the eye is led diagonally from right to left along a footpath by the Tilling Bourne stream, over a wooden bridge, through the gate into the churchyard, to the church framed on either side by trees. To the right of the church and trees in the distance are the houses of Shere village and, beyond, the hill of St Martha's named after the tiny pilgrim's church built on its brow. This hill was a favourite backdrop for landscape artists painting in the area, especially Vicat Cole in the late 1850s.

Colour Plate 48. *A Relic of the Past. Signed and dated 1897. Now 36¼ x 57¾in (originally 43 x 71in) 92 x 146.5cm (originally 109.5 x 180.5cm).* Photograph: Courtesy of Christie's.

Leader's heart went out to her husband, 'Poor Dick! I never felt for anyone more left alone at his age and he so devoted to poor Patty'.[43] Although the painting was intended for the dealer Vokins, he did not purchase it. Possibly he had the same feeling about the content, the tombstones in the churchyard, as Wallis who declined to buy it believing 'the subject was not very popular'. But the painting was well received by Shere parishioners and it was engraved to illustrate the cover of the *Shere Parish Magazine* for a great number of issues from January 1895 onwards (see page 87).[44]

The same parish magazine refers to Leader again in 1896 to congratulate him and his wife on the birth of their daughter, Margaret Isabel, born in March of that year. Leader himself briefly refers to the same event on 23 March, noting that hardly anyone had been to see his Royal Academy paintings before they were sent to London as he 'could ask nobody to the house my wife being upstairs with a baby and the girls having measles one after another'.

Another Surrey subject worthy of mention is 'A Relic from the Past', 1897 (Colour Plate 48, pages 88 and 89), showing the old Malt House (now Malt House Cottages) at Gomshall, dating back to the sixteenth. century. Although Leader has allowed himself artistic licence in the foreground, the house itself, with its notable chimneys and ornate timber framing, is little altered today. Whilst 'A Relic of the Past' passed straight into a private collection, thereby escaping critical appraisal, reviews of Leader's exhibited works throughout the 1890s continued along similar lines to those recorded at the French Gallery during the winter of 1890/91. His works were both praised and criticised, depending on the taste of the fickle critic. Even though he had adopted a much broader and looser style, Leader was seen not to have made any concessions to the French Landscape School as many of the younger British landscape artists were doing. Artists such as David Murray, Joseph Farquharson, Alfred Parsons and Alfred East, now represented a 'New British Landscape School'. It had been a position occupied by Leader thirty years before, but in the late 1890s he was being firmly placed by the critics in the 'Old Landscape School'. This relegation by the critics, despite the popularity of his works among the public, must have added to the increasing frustration felt by Leader in not yet being elected a Royal Academician.

In 1894, when he had to go to London for an election of three Associates, he wrote in his Diary that he was very reluctant to go because not only was he very busy with commissions but he was also '. . . not in a good humour with the Academy. They have not treated me well keeping me an associate after forty years exhibiting with them' (8 January). The election of the portrait painter John Singer Sargent to RA in 1897, after only three years as an Associate, caused Leader to write that he was '. . . depressed and out of heart at my treatment by the Academy having time after time come up for election and rejected each time' (21 March, 1897).

By then he had already been superseded by seven Associates of whom four were painters. In spite of his grievance against the Royal Academy he hosted the annual picnic of the Royal Academy Club in the summer at Burrows Cross House at which thirty-seven members attended. Perhaps Leader mentioned his continual disappointment during this congenial gathering because at the next election of Royal Academicans his ultimate ambition was achieved. After mentioning the pictures he had sent to the 1898 Royal Academy Exhibition and for Tooth's Spring Exhibition, and noting that one of his paintings ('In the evening there shall be light'), which was sold after the death of Sir John Pender the previous autumn, fetched the highest price, £1,205, at Christie's for that year by a living artist, Leader concluded, in an almost casual manner:

> In February (the 3rd I think) I was at last elected
> R.A . . . It is a matter of great satisfaction for me
> for I was getting sore with the Academy and that
> feeling would have increased if my election had been
> postponed. Seymour Lucas was my chief opponent he
> came in after me.[45]   (24 March, 1898)

Sunset Years
1899-1923

The Council of the Royal Academy 1907. Photographic reproduction of the finished painting by Hubert Von Herkomer. B.W.L. is seated fourth from the left.
Courtesy of the Royal Academy of Arts, London.

Leader's reason for ending his Diaries so abruptly, with the announcement of his election to Royal Academician, was probably because he felt they were no longer necessary. In achieving his ultimate ambition of full membership there was no longer the need for him to pen his grievances towards the Royal Academy. He would now have a voice in the institution's future policies when taking his turn, on a rotational basis, on the Royal Academy Council. A photogravure of 'The Council of the Royal Academy 1907', depicts its members, including Leader fourth from the left, judging pictures for that year's Summer Exhibition. The President, Sir Edward John Poynter (1836-1919), eighth from the left, holds the metal letters, D (doubtful) and X (excluded) and the artist of the original painting which was exhibited at the Royal Academy in 1908, No.391, Hubert von Herkomer (1849-1914), is seated second from the right in front of the sculptor Sir Thomas Brock (1847-1922).[1]

With the coveted letters, 'RA' after his name, the on-going popularity of Leader's paintings and his financial success were assured. (At the end of 1898 Leader had recorded in his Account Books that the sale of his paintings, plus investment dividends, for that year totalled £7,126.16s. 7d. or the equivalent of £360,000 today). With the exception of the occasional private commission, the artist was now, and would be in the future, selling his paintings only through the art dealers. Because of the unabated demand for his work, he could allow himself the luxury of painting what he liked. Unfortunately, this led to much repetition of earlier subjects which have been condemned today as 'commercial landscapes'. This was the case for the majority of Leader's paintings executed during his latter years. But it must be said in his defence that, for an ageing gentleman who would not be able to go about the countryside in search of new subjects as nimbly as he had in his youth, he still had a keen eye and the artistic facility to continue to produce original works alongside his more repetitious productions.

As with all artists when elected to Royal Academician, Leader had to present a specimen of his work to the Royal Academy. After it had been approved by the Council, he would then receive a 'Letter of Administration', or Diploma, signed by the monarch, Queen Victoria. Leader's Diploma painting was 'The Sand Pit, Burrows Cross' (Colour Plate 49, page 92) exhibited at the Royal Academy, No.23, in 1899. This painting is a true specimen of Leader's finished studio work, containing many compositional features which can be found in his landscapes

Colour Plate 49. *The Sand Pit, Burrows Cross. Signed and dated 1898. 24 x 40in (61 x 101.5cm).* Photograph: Courtesy of the Royal Academy of Arts, London.

dating from the 1860s. Of course, there are variations, but these were based on a general theme depending on both the amount of artistic licence chosen to create a well-balanced composition and the type of landscape selected. Adaptations were made to match the geography of the location, such as the mountainous landscapes of Wales and Switzerland, the flat plains of Worcestershire, the gently rolling hills of Surrey or the expansive coast lines of North Wales and Sussex.

The Diploma work (above) is a summer scene depicting the late afternoon, a favoured time of the day with Leader, in a sand pit on the common close to his home. St Martha's Hill and The Chantries wood are in the far distance. His customary small unobtrusive figures, the men loading sand onto their horse-drawn cart in the pit and the group with a collie dog walking along the track above, whilst adding interest to the scene, have been specifically positioned as an aid for perspective purposes. The organisation of the composition is, in many respects, typical of Leader. It has been divided almost horizontally in half between the sky and the landscape and as was customary with him the horizon line is broken. Here there is an irregular diagonal line of trees, the most dominant feature in the middle distance, which slopes away from the right leaving the left side scene open to an extended vista. Whichever side of a canvas Leader selected to place the higher horizon line almost invariably became the main focus of the scene, but 'The Sand Pit, Burrows Cross' is not typical in this respect as the sand pit containing the men with the horse-drawn cart is the main focal point. Whilst the unity of this scene is, in part, achieved by the structure of the composition, the method of painting which Leader had increasingly employed since the 1870s also plays an important role. This includes more regard for masses rather than an accentuation of details and bold brushstrokes from a limited warmer palette. These, combined, enhance the overall natural effects of a late afternoon where the sun shines on the tops of the trees and the distant hill. The only colour contrasts are the small areas of white paint, embracing the clothing and the horse, and red highlights on the cart wheels and on the jacket of the middle man. These are perspective devices - focal points, leading one's eye into the scene - Leader had borrowed from Constable's landscapes. Leader also often used patches of bright highlights in the middle distance of a scene to achieve the same purpose.

The artist's most consistent media supporter, *The Art Journal*, which believed it had done much to promote Leader since the 1860s, took the opportunity to congratulate him on his recent election as RA. This took the form of an extensive monograph on Leader published in their *Christmas Art Annual* for 1901. In the announcement of the forthcoming monograph, the Editor and the Proprietors of *The Art Journal* declared that they wished to show their appreciation of an artist who was ' one of the most truly national painters which the British Isles have ever produced'[2] whose works, in their opinion, were a 'national product worthy of the country which has produced Constable, Cox, and Crome'.[3] Lewis Lusk, who had studied under John Ruskin when at Oxford, was commissioned to write the monograph which, consistent with the publishers' views, was more an appreciation of Leader's paintings than an in-depth critique or analysis. Lusk was clearly in sympathy with Leader's own affinity to, and portrayal of, Worcestershire. He too had experienced the unique 'amber luminosity' of that part of Britain and praised Leader's 'fidelity to that quality'. He also observed in Leader's paintings the artist's facility to adjust the effects of light according to the atmospheric conditions which varied from region to region.

In spite of the then current avant-garde and fashionable view held by artists and critics of an Anglo-Parisian bias that art should not be symbolic or illustrative, Lusk was not afraid to compare, in flowery prose, what he believed was the lyrical sentiment expressed in some of Leader's Worcestershire landscapes with the landscape poetry of George Meredith[4] and George Herbert.[5] He also referred to his own favourite Leader painting 'The Old Holyhead Road', dated 1885. He said it had 'the sentiment of a great epic, or one of Sir Walter Scott's more sombre romances'[6] because it was a portrait of a retired National Servant which once carried the Royal Mail from London to Ireland via Holyhead but, having been superseded by the railway, was left in solitude.

As regards the biographical content, there is no doubt Lusk only wrote as much as Leader told him, and that was only what the artist wished his public to know. This included a reiteration of Dafforne's 1871 biographical details of Leader's early life,[7] namely, an image of child 'prodigy' and self-taught artist who, relatively separated from the competitive pressures of exhibiting, had doggedly pursued his own style of painting to become extremely successful. Such a portrait would have been much appreciated by many of the Victorian readers who were themselves successful self-made men.

The monograph was well illustrated with Leader's paintings, covering the period from the 1850s to 1901, and with photographs of Burrows Cross House. Those of the interior show a

Burrows Cross House, from the south. Photograph: *Art Annual* 1901. Supplement of 'Art Journal', page 28.

The Studio, Burrows Cross House.
Photograph: Art Annual 1901, supplement of *Art Journal,* page 30.

The Drawing-room, Burrows Cross House.
Photograph: *Art Annual* 1901. Supplement of 'Art Journal', page 29.

The Hall, Burrows Cross House.
Photograph: *Art Annual* 1901, supplement of 'Art Journal', page 29.

B.W. Leader at Whittington Lodge. Family Photograph.

great number of paintings hanging on the walls. In addition to retaining works by himself, and by his wife, Leader had accumulated a large collection of landscapes by British and Continental artists dating from the eighteenth century onwards, works that emphasise his commitment to, and admiration for, the tradition of landscape painting. Surrounded by such works was, no doubt, a constant inspiration for him. These paintings included a woody scene with shepherd and sheep by Gainsborough, 'Willy Lott's House' by Constable,[8] 'The Brook' painted by J. Linnell Sen. in 1854, and a small David Cox watercolour. There were also landscapes by his contemporaries and friends such as David Murray, Alfred Parsons and Sidney Richard Percy. Landscapes from the Continent included several examples of modern Dutch work painted in broad pure colouring. Among the works by French artists were Ch. Jacque's 'The Flock' and W. Bouguereau's 'The Shepherdess', 1868, and a landscape by the Italian Salvator Rosa. Leader also owned a Fantin–Latour still life and 'The Forsaken' by an artist celebrated for his paintings of the female nude, William Etty.[9] A large painting, 'The Herb Gatherers' by Pierre Billet[10] acquired while residing at Whittington Lodge had taken pride of place over a fireplace (see above).

The subject matter of one of the paintings in the collection was copied by Leader. Dated 1901, he acknowledged his debt to the artist of the original painting by inscribing the stretcher of his (Leader's) version 'Willy Lott's House; the subject of Constable' (Colour Plate 50, page 96). Unlike his father's deliberate copy of 'Gillingham Mill', painted over half a century before (see page 12, 'Background and Formative Years'), Leader's painting could never be mistaken for a 'Constable', nor was intended to be. Whilst Constable's 'Willy Lott's House' displays the rapid execution of a *plein air* sketch in an almost expressionistic manner of broad masses of light and shade in limited sombre tones, like a personal notation. Leader's painting, also small, is a carefully composed and balanced studio work. The scene has been extended either side to

Colour Plate 50. *Willy Lott's House. Signed and dated 1901. 12 x 18in (30.5 x 46cm).*

Photograph: Courtesy of Sotheby's.

Colour Plate 51. *A Quiet Evening. Signed and dated 1904. 48 x 72in (122 x 183cm).*

Photograph: Courtesy of Richard Green, London.

B.W. Leader, 1901. Photograph: Courtesy of Frost & Reed, London.

B.W. Leader with his terrier, Burrows Cross House. Photograph: Private Collection.

Mary Eastlake. Photograph: Private Collection.

include more of the house and the right bank of the stream than can be seen in Constable's sketch. The stream itself has been given greater prominence flowing between the wooded banks to where it meets the River Stour in the distance. The style, like the majority of Leader's small landscapes at this time, is impressionistic in its apparent lack of finish and touches of bright colour.

In the same year, 1901, Leader exhibited three paintings at the Royal Academy Summer Exhibition. Two of these, 'An Old Southern Port', No.445 (Colour Plate 52, page 98) and 'Our South Coast', No.458, were both scenes at Littlehampton in Sussex. Now that he was living in Surrey, Littlehampton, rather than the Welsh coast, became the favoured seaside resort for the family during the summer. Once a thriving sea-faring port at the mouth of the Arun River, before its decline at the end of the nineteenth century, Littlehampton was the destination for the large sailing ships carrying wood and coal mainly from the Baltic, Sweden, Norway and Russia. It was also the departure point for sailing ships built in the harbour's shipyard. The South Coast Railway Company built a line into the town in 1863 and not only did it operate a cross-channel ferry to Normandy but it also brought the holiday makers to enjoy the miles of sandy beaches lined with deep sand dunes.

The Leader family stayed in one of the many large seafront Georgian houses on the South Terrace east of the old Port which served as accommodation for the more wealthy visitors with their servants. There is no record of when the family first stayed at Littlehampton but Leader's small oil sketches of the location date from 1896. A dated pencil sketch of the church at Bury (below), north of the resort, is evidence that the artist visited the Arun Valley four years earlier. From this sketch, dated 24 May, 1892, Leader produced an oil painting titled 'Amberley on the Arun', 1894,[11] which is now in the Cincinnati Art Gallery, Ohio, U.S.A. It depicts the church of St John the Evangelist, the Manor and the farm at Bury from the Amberley side of the Arun at the point of the Bury ferry crossing.[12]

The ferry boat, in front of one of the Manor farm cottages, is depicted in the foreground of the painting. In style and subject matter the painting is very similar to those of the riverside villages along the Severn below Worcester. If the title was not inscribed on the reverse in the artist's hand the painting would be mistaken for a Severn landscape. Leader exhibited a larger version of the scene, employing greater artistic licence, at the 1904 Royal Academy, No.168, giving it a non-locational title of 'A Quiet Evening' (Colour Plate 51). Other subjects in the area include a small oil sketch of Arundel Castle from the Arun in 1896.

Pencil sketch of 'The Church and Manor House at Bury'.
Photograph: Courtesy of Frost & Reed, London.

Colour Plate 52. *An Old Southern Port. Signed and dated 1901. 44 x 72in (112 x 183cm).* Photograph: Courtesy of Richard Green, London.

Whilst the majority of Leader's Sussex coastal paintings are of undulating sand dunes, dotted with blue sea thistles and grasses, and calm seas, similar in subject to his Welsh coastal scenes, there are also a few of significant historical interest. These include 'An Old Southern Port' (Colour Plate 52), the subject of which is Littlehampton harbour in its sunset years. Although it was an original subject for the artist, it was painted with the confidence of a master. In fact, the painting is like an 'old master' in appearance due to Leader's predominant use of warm browns to depict the scene lit by the glow of the late afternoon sun. The eye is led diagonally into the scene along the stony water's edge past the small rowing craft alongside the paddle harbour tug 'Jumna' tied to the Piles. Beyond, in the middle distance, two full-rigged sailing ships are tied against decaying wooden quays discharging their cargoes. Other sailing ships placed strategically along the quays lead us along the River Arun to the distant rise of the South Downs. In accordance with the artist's usual practice there are preliminary sketches of the scene made of the spot. These include a detailed pencil sketch of the tug 'Jumna'. He also produced a smaller version of his Royal Academy picture.

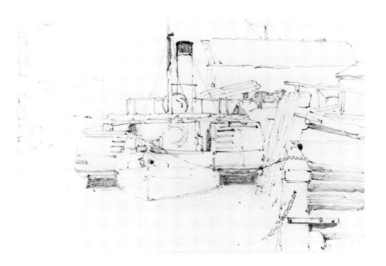

Pencil sketch of 'The Tug "Jumna"'. (Colour Plate 52). Photograph: Courtesy of Frost & Reed, London.

The picturesque harbour had been the subject for artists such as G. Poulson and John Constable in the first half of the nineteenth century. The London-based landscape and genre painter, Sydney Pike (fl.1880-1901), chose the same view as Leader about the same time,[13] and the harbour was also painted by one of the greatest British marine painters of this century, Leslie Arthur Wilcox (1908 –1982).[14]

Leader's other Sussex scene exhibited at the 1901 Royal Academy, 'Our South Coast', is of a view to the west of the harbour entrance. The painting depicts the golf links, separated from the sea in the lee of the sand dunes, with Climping windmill in the distance. Another windmill which once stood at the harbour entrance where the pier, or jetty, begins is depicted by Leader in a small oil sketch (Colour Plate 53) as a backdrop to a travelling circus on 'The Green', in front of the South Terrace. This windmill had also featured in 'Stormy Effect, Littlehampton'[15] painted by John Constable in July 1835 during one of his visits to friends, the Constable family of Arundel (no relation). Constable loved the scenery of the Arun valley and commented on it in at least one of his letters to George Constable.[16]

It is noticeable that, while the Sussex and Welsh coastlines are well represented in Leader's *oeuvre* as a result of continual visits, there are relatively few paintings featuring the coastline and

Colour Plate 53. *Funfair, Littlehampton. Board. Signed and dated 1907. 12½ x 17¼in (32 x 44cm).* Private Collection.

landscape of Devon and Cornwall. Although this can be partly explained by an early comment by Leader in 1865, after returning from an Autumn's visit to north Devon, that he 'did no work, not caring for the scenery' (Diary, 20 December, 1865), a few paintings of the county have come to light. These were mostly painted in the 1870s and 1880s and depicted the moors and vales around Dartmoor. Examples are 'A Fine Day on Dartmoor', 1878, (Colour Plate 54, page 102) and 'On the Borders of Dartmoor', 1881, (Colour Plate 55, page 103). It is also apparent, due to the absence of inland scenes of Cornwall, that Leader did not care for the Cornish landscape. In a letter to his daughter Mary he wrote that it was 'so shut in with hills, no distance unless you got to the tops and then it was too extensive for my kind of work' (20 November, 1910).

Of the West Country coastline, there are those known pictures painted 'Near Tintagel' (Colour Plate 24, page 45) and of 'St Michael's Mount' (Colour Plate 30, page 52) in the 1870s, then apparently nothing until about 1900 when Leader painted scenes of Mount Edgecomb, near Plymouth. His first Royal Academy painting of this region, but further west, was 'The Incoming Tide on the Cornish Coast' (Colour Plate 56, page 103) exhibited in 1905, No.485. This scene of a secluded sandy cove nestling beneath rocky cliffs and occupied by a single group of figures, drew praise from *The Art Journal* reviewer because he felt that its veteran artist, then seventy-four years old, had so realistically reminded the 'seaside tourist' of the real thing.[17] Two later Royal Academy exhibits, 1912 and 1917, were of Porth, near Newquay.

Perhaps it is not surprising that there are so few paintings of the West Country even though, after Leader's marriage, frequent trips were made to Plymouth to visit his wife's family, the Eastlakes. As a consequence of the uneasy relationship between the artist and his relations-in-law, it seems likely that these visits were 'duty' visits for Leader, with little time (and probably little inclination) for sketching excursions. A letter headed 'The Grand Hotel, Plymouth', to his daughter Mary, who was looking after Burrows Cross House while Leader and his wife were staying in Plymouth during World War I, seems to confirm Leader's ordeal. He wrote it was a 'trial' visiting the relatives because 'Mummy won't go alone'.[18] To make matters worse, the weather for May was 'wretchedly bad' that particular year.

Mary has been the first of the children to marry. In 1906, she married Lieutenant-Colonel Tringham in St Martha's Church (the church on the distant hill in 'Shere Church', Colour Plate 43, page 84). Her elder sister, Ethel, the only other daughter to marry, was married in 1915 in Shere Church to Roland James May, a civil engineer from Norfolk. Edward, Leader's second son, did not take up the paint brush like his brother Benjamin, becoming instead a barrister at the Inner Temple. His early athletic prowess gained him an Athletics Blue while at Trinity College, Cambridge and led to him representing his country in the High Jump and Hurdles at the 1908 Olympic Games. Edward married into an artistic family, close neighbours of the Leaders. In 1914 he married Alice, one of the daughters of the genre painter and watercolourist Frank William Warwick Topham (1838-1924). When Topham moved with his family from Hampstead in London to Pitch Hill, Holmbury St Mary, Surrey in 1890 there was already a small community of artists in residence there. The landscape painter John Clayton Adams (1840-1906) had lived there since 1872. Lusk had mentioned the artist's friendship with Leader and Leader's other friends who were the portrait painter and miniaturist Henry Tanworth Wells RA (1828-1903) and the landscape painter Frank Walton (1840-1928). Both artists resided at Holmbury St Mary - Wells since the 1860s and Walton from 1872. Other 'Pitch Hill' artists, doubtless acquainted with Leader, were the Worcestershire landscape painter George William Mote (1832-1909), John Sparkes (died 1907) and his wife Catherine. Although these successful artists, who were all of Leader's generation and on the same social level had, like him, built or purchased large houses in close proximity to each other, there is no evidence which has come to light, either written or verbal, of the extent to which Leader socialised with them.

As mentioned earlier, Leader was very much committed to his work and family. At this late stage in his life his commitment to both had not diminished rather it had increased with his additional duties as a full member of the Royal Academy and as head of his extending family. Respect for this dedicated veteran from within London's artistic community led to Leader becoming one of the patrons, along with such artists as the Royal Academicians Edwin Austin Abbey (1852-1911), James Jebusa Shannon (1862-1823), and Frank Cadogan Cowper (1877-1958) of The Byam Shaw and Vicat Cole School of Art in Campden Hill, founded in 1910.[19] (Vicat Cole [Reginald Rex], 1870-1940, was the son of Leader's old departed friend, George).

By this time, Leader had also achieved international fame, especially across the Atlantic. His landscapes were entering both public and private collections. Individual collectors from America and Canada had been purchasing his paintings on their visits to Britain since Currie, from Philadelphia, acquired Leader's first Royal Academy exhibit in 1854. From the 1880s the dealer Tooth had prints of Leader's most popular Royal Academy paintings published in these countries. However, with the demand for Leader's landscapes growing, his dealer, Wallis, was sending them straight from the easel to art dealers in the cities of Detroit, Boston, Montreal, Toronto, and Ottawa.[20] The growth of the art market in America and Canada for British and continental art was, no doubt, stimulated by the success of the Chicago Art Exhibition at their World's Fair in 1893. (Two landscapes by Leader were exhibited). This, in turn, provided the stimulus for the Ontario Society of Arts to stage their own art exhibitions at the Canadian National Exhibition held from 1905 until 1938. Leader's 'Fast Falls the Eventide', an 1897 Royal Academy painting, was loaned to the 1909 Exhibition by its owner, the Corporation of Liverpool while other contemporary British landscapes included those by Alfred Parsons and Henry Moore. On this side of the Atlantic, in Ireland, other Corporations namely, of Blackburn, London and Southport loaned their Leader paintings to the 1902 Cork International Exhibition.[21]

Leader's spreading fame as one of the leading and most popular British landscape artists extended beyond the public who viewed his pictures at exhibitions or purchased his paintings and engravings. Numerous articles on his work and career appeared in national and local journals such as *The Strand* and *The Windsor* magazines. He was even sufficiently well-known to the public to rate a mention in E.M. Forster's *Howards End*, first published 1910. His character Margaret Schegel, while admiring the visionary qualities which the Swiss artist Arnold Brocklin (1827-1901) attempted to imbue into his landscape, had to concede that they 'don't come off' as the tangible landscapes by Leader 'do'.[22] Leader was also included with other distinguished British personalities in an advertisement for the tonic 'Sanatogen' in the widely read *Illustrated London News*.[23] His photograph, along with nine other celebrities, including the novelists Hall Caine, Edward Frederic Benson and Sarah Grand, the playwright Henry Arthur Jones and the composer and conductor Landon Ronald, was printed along with an autographed comment on the product. For Leader, his recovery from a severe attack of congestion of the lungs (he was a heavy cigar smoker) was attributed to his having regularly taken the tonic.

At the time of the advertisement dark clouds of war were gathering over Europe, but two events during the first half of 1914 relating to Leader's prominent position in English landscape painting would have been regarded by him with pride. First, was the purchase of one of his Royal Academy pictures that year 'On the Llugwy, Bettws-y-coed', No.3, by King George V and Queen Mary. The painting was the first by Leader to enter the Royal Collection. Probably because none of his landscapes had been bought by Queen Victoria his comments regarding Her Majesty were none too flattering and included his belief that she had bad taste in art. A later Royal commission, painted in the last year of his life, was a miniature watercolour of pine trees for Queen Mary's Doll's House.[24]

It does seem appropriate that in the same year that Their Majesties purchased Leader's painting he should be honoured on the King's birthday, 3 June, by the citizens of Worcester giving him the Freedom of the City.[25] Although the recognition was rather belated (both the

Colour Plate 54. *A Fine Day on Dartmoor. Signed and dated 1878. 20 x 30in (51 x 76cm).* Photograph: Courtesy of Richard Green, London.

composer Sir Edward Elgar and the sculptor Sir Thomas Brock RA having received the honour some years earlier), the people of Worcester had shown that their third famous artistic 'son' was not forgotten. The occasion was celebrated by a luncheon given by the Mayor in Worcester's Guildhall, where Leader was presented with a casket in the form of a porcelain inkstand, with an inscribed silver plaque in the shape of a scroll, on the ivory base, announcing he was a freeman. The casket, in the Italian Renaissance style of the fifteenth century, was made at the Worcester Royal Porcelain Works[26] where Leader had once been a Director. Sir Edward Elgar was among the distinguished guests present who paid tribute to Leader by

Inkstand presented to B.W. Leader in 1914 when given the Freedom of the City of Worcester. Private Collection.

13. Ibid., p.19.

14. Paintings exhibited Worcester 1834. 'Salisbury Cathedral-from the Bishop's Grounds', No.26, 'Landscape - A Barge passing a Lock on the Stour', No.141. Constable sent five paintings in 1835 and nine in 1836. See Parris, I. and Fleming-Williams, I. *Constable,* Tate Gallery Publications, 1991 for the exhibition of 13 June - 15 September, 1991. pp.41-42.

15. 'Gillingham Mill',1823-1827. Exhibited Worcester 1835, No.68.

16. Windsor, Lord. *John Constable R.A.,* 'The Makers of British Art Series', The Walter Scott Publishing Co. Ltd., London, 1903. p.137.

17. Other known paintings exhibited by E.L. Williams in 1836 were 'Tewkesbury from the Lower Lode Ferry', No.57 and 'Recollection of Ventnor Cove, Isle of Wight', No.71. In 1838, 'Sharpness Point, The Junction of Gloucester and Berkeley Ship Canal with River Severn', No.99.

18. In the possession of B.W. Leader until his death in 1923.

19. *Berrows Worcester Journal*, 24 March, 1923, p.4. Leader was reported to have written this in 1905. He did not write this in the *Berrows Worcester Journal* at any time in 1905 (original source unknown). Dunstable was one of the areas where the manufacture of straw hats was a thriving cottage industry in the nineteenth century.

20. Beckett, R.B. *John Constable's Discourses,* Vol.XIV, Suffolk Records Society, 1970, p.30.

21. Ibid., p.32.

22. Diary, 18 February, 1889.

23. Op. cit. *Berrows Worcester Journal.*

24. Frederick Dolman *An Artist's Life-Work; A Morning with Mr. B.W. Leader A.R.A.,* published by *The Quiver Magazine,* 1897, p.100.

25. Op. cit. Lusk, p.13.

26. Op. cit. *Berrows Worcester Journal.*

27. Mr. Williams became a member of the Institution of Civil Engineers 30 June, 1846. Source: *The Institution of Civil Engineers. Form 880-2Y.* Source: *Commercial Directory for Gloucester, Hereford, and Worcester. 1851 Census* - E.L. Williams, Civil Engineer M.I.C.E.

28. Thomas Rhodes was appointed consulting engineer.

29. Modified plans, to reduce the opposition, were re-introduced to Parliament in 1938 but had to be withdrawn.

30. An Act was passed to improve the River Severn and to levy tolls. The compromise consisted of the construction of a series of locks and weirs from Worcester north to Stourport with dredging south to Gloucester. Flooding and silting still occurred south of Worcester so in 1852, at vast expense, the construction of a lock and weir at Upper Lode, Tewkesbury was begun. By 1872 this lock and weir and those near Gloucester, which were in Mr.Williams' original plans, were finally built.

31. No record of this is held at the Institution of Civil Engineers. It was reported in the *Berrows Worcester Journal,* March, 1879, p.5.

32. Williams, E.L. *On Land Drainage and Irrigation and on the Application of Drainage water as a motive power to machinery for Agricultural Purposes,* London, 1849. Copy held by the British Museum Library, London. Papers by E.L. Williams relating to the Severn Navigation Commission are held at the Institution of Civil Engineers.

33. Now called the Diglis House Hotel.

34. Op. cit. Lusk, p.14.

35. Follett, F.V., *A History of the Worcester Royal Grammar School*, published by Ebenezer Baylis, The Trinity Press, Worcester and London, 1951. pp.66 & 192. Called 'Queen Elizabeth's Grammar School' until 1869 when the school, on a new site, was granted the title 'Royal' by Queen Victoria.

36. Op. cit., *Berrows Worcester Journal.*

37. Op. cit., Follett pp.74–75, 192, 201–202. Benjamin Leader's attendance at the Worcester Royal Grammar School is recorded from 1841-1845.

38. Letter headed 'Silver Street Academy' dated 6 December, 1843, from Benjamin to his parents mentioning the Christmas vacation and Mr. and Mrs. Colville the couple who ran the Academy.

39. *Berrows Worcester Journal*, 6 June, 1914, p.3.

40. Letter dated 20 April, 1995 from A.W. Potter, Information Assistant, Royal Academy of Arts, London.

41. Ibid.

42. Op.cit. *Berrows Worcester Journal*, 24 March, 1923.

43. It was only called the 'Summer Exhibition' from the early

1870s. Previously it was the 'Exhibition of the Works of Living Artists'. Source: Hutchison, S.C. *The History of the Royal Academy 1768-1986*, Robert Ryce Ltd., London, 1986. p.115.

44. Op.cit., *Berrows Worcester Journal*, 24 March 1923.

45. From the 'Minutes Book' of the Worcester Society of Arts 1853. Held at the Worcester Reference Library.

46. Ibid. 'Minutes Book' 28 February, 1866

47. *Edgbastonia*, II, 58 (34824) April 1882, pp.58-61. *Birmingham Post*, 14 March, 1882.

48. King, L.S. *The Industrialization of Taste, Victorian England and The Art Union of London*, UMI Research Press, Michigan, USA, 1980, p.238.

49. This could be Henry Brittan Willis RWS (1810-1884), painter of landscapes and cattle and a lithographer.

50. A letter addressed to Carington was sold with the painting at Sotheby's November 20th, 1963, Lot 84. Richard Smith-Carington, B.W. Leader's brother-in-law, died in 1901 and there were no children. The letter could be to a nephew.

51. 'Sally' could have been either Elizabeth, born 1841 or Sabrina, born 1843.

52. Thomas Campbell (1777-1844), Scottish poet. 'The Pleasures of Hope' was first published in 1799. The lines which are appended to the painting begin 'Lo! at the couch where infant beauty sleeps . . .', Line 5, p.19, from *The Pleasures of Hope with Other Poems*, London, 1816.

53. The British Institution, 1806-1867, founded by a number of noblemen and gentlemen, which included Sir George Beaumont, to encourage British Art. It was not intended to rival the Royal Academy as the Institution's annual exhibitions of modern paintings were held at the British Gallery in Pall Mall during February. By the end of the1850s there was much published criticism of the exhibitions with regard to selection, hanging, and in the general display of mediocrity. When the Institution closed the Royal Academy began to have Winter Loan Exhibitions.

54. Ruskin, John. *Modern Painters*, Edited and Abridged by David Barrie, Andre Deutsch, London, 1989, pp.178-179.

BID FOR FAME PART 1: 1857-1862

1. The artist exhibited as 'B. Leader'. Source: 'Catalogue of the Exhibition of the National Institute', Portland Gallery, 316 Regent St., London. 1857, Nos.14, 153, 319, 322.

2. Dafforne, James. 'British Artists: Their Style and Character. No.XCII - Benjamin Williams Leader', printed in the *Art Journal*, February 1871, p.45.

3. Six sons, all painters, were born to Edward Williams, 1782-1855.

4. *The Times*, 1864, 11 February, p.6, col.d.

5. Ibid. 1857, 18 May, p.10, col.d.

6. *The Illustrated London News*, 3 September, 1892, p.312.

7. Ruskin, John. *Academy Notes 1855-1888*, Vol.XIV, p.113.

8. Leader was quoted as saying in 1897 that his painting 'The Bird Trap' (exhibited at the Royal Academy, 1856, No.110) received praise from Ruskin in his *Academy Notes*. Source: F. Dolman, 'An Artist's Life-Work. A Morning with Mr. B.W. Leader A.R.A.', *The Quiver Magazine*, 1897, p.100. There is no mention of the painting in Ruskin's *Academy Notes, 1856*'.

9. *The Saturday Review*, 1857, p.451.

10. Baldry, A.L. *Sir John Everett Millais: His Art and Influence*, George Bell & Sons, London, 1899. p.46.

11. Op cit. *The Saturday Review*, 19 May, 1888, p.625.

12. Diary, April 1858.

13. For more information see S.C. Hutchison's *The History of the Royal Academy 1768-1986*, Robert Ryce Ltd., London, 1986.

14. Ibid., p.117 and Notes, p.235.

15. Diary, 6 November, 1858.

16. Ibid.

17. Diary, 9 February, 1859.

18. There is a landscape dated 1856 and another dated 1857 of the River Conway at Betws-y-coed which has a sketch relating to it. These are evidence that Leader visited Wales earlier and did not mention it.

19. *The Athenaeum*, No.1639, 26 March, 1859, p.426.

20. 'The Warren Gate, Albury', No.560. Portland Gallery (National Institute). 'The Wood in Surrey', No.403. P.G. (N.I.) 'The Heath at Albury', No.10. Royal Academy.

21. Chignell, Robert, *The Life and Paintings of George Vicat Cole R.A.*, 1898.

22. Holiday, H. *Reminiscences of my Life,* published 1914, p.79.

23. Ibid.

24. Today the painting is hanging in the reception area of the Royal Oak Hotel which was rebuilt 1861–62 and has been extended since.

25. E489, 496 – 1969, from the Album of 110 sketches by B.W. Leader. Held at the Victoria & Albert Museum (Print Room), London. Access No.E437 – 550 – 1969. Press No.94.13.30.

26. The conifers were planted by the Forestry Commission in the early 1920s to meet the demand of industry for quick-grown supplies of timber.

27. The painting was attributed to both artists when sold by Christie's in Rome, 12 December, 1988, Lot 281.

28. B. Disraeli, *Coningsby* published by Blackie & Son, London, p.157.

29. *Kilvert's Diary 1870-1879: Selection from the Diary of the Rev. Francis Kilvert,* Chosen, Edited and Introduced by William Plomer, Penguin Books, 1977, pp.187-9, 233, 267.

30. Herbert Ingram, 1811–1860. His son, Sir William Ingram, 1862-1924, Managing Director of the I.L.N. and *The Sketch,* also purchased paintings by Leader: see Appendix 3.

31. *The Illustrated London News,* Supplement 2 June, 1860, No.1034, Vol.XXXVI.

32. Ibid.

33. Founded 1838. Source: *Langham Sketching Club Exhibition Catalogue, 1887,* Introduction. Held at the National Art Library, Victoria and Albert Museum. It is not known how long Leader was a member. He exhibited a painting 'Evening', No.44, at the Club's exhibition in 1887 held at Arthur Vokins Gallery, 23 Baker St., London.

34. Originally the Society and Club occupied premises at Chipstow St., Fitzroy Sq. Source: Story, Alfred T. *A Bohemian Artist's Club;* pub'd. in *The Strand Magazine,* May 1894, pp.488-496.

BID FOR FAME PART 2: 1863-1870
1. Gassiot bequeathed his collection of paintings, including Leader's Welsh scene, then called 'A Welsh Churchyard, Bettws-y-coed', to the Corporation of London. At the time of writing the painting is on loan to the Palace of Westminster.

2. *The Art Journal* Vol.II, 1863, 1 June, pp.105–116.

3. Ibid. Vol.III, 1864, June, p.166.

4. *The Times,* 1864, 30 April, p.14, col.b.

5. Ibid.

6. *The Art Journal,* Vol.IV, 1865, June, p.170.

7. Ibid.

8. Diary, 22 July, 1865.

9. Op. cit. *The Art Journal,* 1865, p.171. The reviewer's description of 'Autumn's Last Gleam' was actually of 'A Sunny Afternoon, North Wales', No.317.

10. Ibid.

11. Diary, 22 July, 1865.

12. *The Times,* 1923, 23 March, p.15, col.e.

13. Minutes held at The Royal Academy archives. Elected to Associates were the sculptor, Joseph Durham, 1814–1877; architect, George Edmund St., 1844–1881; and three painters, Erskine Nicol, 1825-1904, John Pettie, 1839-1893 and Henry Tanworth Wells, 1828-1903.

14. The next time Leader's name appeared in the Minutes was in January 1870. He then received two votes.

15. Diary, 21 May, 1866.

16. Ibid.

17. *The Times,* 1866, 12 June, p.6, col.c.

18. Ibid.

19. David Price, 1809-1891. Boyes, J.F. *The Private Art Collections of London: The Late Mr. David Price's,* in Queen Anne St. Published in *The Art Journal,* November 1891, pp.321-328.

20. 'Dernier Rayon de l'Automne', No.80.

21. Diary, 3 July, 1867.

22. Ibid.

23. This was reported to the author by one of Leader's grand-daughters.

24. *The Art Journal,* 1871, p.47.

25. Ibid.

26. Ibid. pp.45-47

27. Letters from Leader to Hall are held at the Worcestershire County Records Office.

BID FOR FAME PART 3: 1871–1882

1. In 1885 Sir Robert became Lord Monkwell.

2. *The Art Journal* Vol.XII, 1873, p.238.

3. An earlier association with the Royal Academy was in giving evidence to the 1863 Royal Commission. This was set up to enquire into the position of the RA in relation to the Fine Arts, the circumstances and conditions which it occupied, at the time, part of the National Gallery. It was also to suggest measures that might be required to render it more useful in promoting Art and to improve and develop public taste. This was because whilst the RA accepted public financing it acted as if it were a private institution. Brodhurst (1886) *The Royal Academy*. Source: J. Penderel – *Inquests and Commissions. The Magazine of Art,* 1886, Vol.IX, pp.382-384.

4. *The Times,* 26 May, 1874, p.8, col.a.

5. Ibid.

6. Ibid. 15 May, 1875, p.12, col.c.

7. Diary, 10 September, 1876.

8. Ibid. 13 December, 1872.

9. A position he held from 1851 until his death.

10. This was to be repaid at 4% per annum subject to six months notice on either side. Source: Minutes of Directors' Meeting, 1885, 14 December, Minute 3457. Mr. Beale, Leader's acting solicitor, 15 Foregate St., Worcester.

11. Diary, 11 January, 1877.

12. Op cit. Lusk, p.25.

13. *The Athenaeum,* No.2205, 29 January, 1870, p.156.

14. Diary, 1877, 18 February and 8 March.

15. Diary, 1887, 1 July. This could be the landscape painter David Cox Jr. (1809-1885), the only child of David Cox. He exhibited from 1827-1884 at the various London venues but had only three works exhibited at the Royal Academy.

Possibly Daniel Muller (fl.1863-1858), landscape and figurative painter. Exhibited four landscapes at the Royal Academy.

16. This painting of the River Bruan, 56 x 82in (142 x 208cm), was a direct commission from the art patron David Price (see 'Bid for Fame, Part 2, 1863-1870', p.39).

17. Diary, 1 July, 1887.

18. *The Art Journal,* Vol.XVL, 1877, p.269.

19. *The Times,* 22 May, 1877, p.11, col.a.

20. 'Aiguille Verte', No.971.

21. Diary, 23 January, 1878.

22. Diary, 1 April, 1878.

23. Diary, 7 May, 1878.

24. *The Art Journal,* 1879, p.13.

25. *The Illustrated London News,* 1878, October-December, p.423.

26. *The Times,* 1878, 5 November, p.8, col.a.

27. Diary, 24 January, 1879.

28. All the following artists exhibited at the Royal Academy but never became members:-
Possibly David Cox Snr. RWS, (1781-1859). Painter of landscapes, coastal scenes, and rustic genre, or his son David Cox Jnr. (1801-1885). Daniel Muller (Already mentioned, Note 15).
Possibly the landscape painter, Patrick Nasmyth (1787-1831). Eldest of eleven children of the Scottish landscape painter, Alexander Nasmyth. John Berney Crome (1794–1842). Norwich School. Landscape painter.
This could be William Linnell (1826-1906), landscape and rustic genre painter, or John Linnell (1792-1882) who also painted landscapes.
This could be Henry Dawson (1811-1878), marine and landscape painter, or his son Alfred (fl.1860-1890), landscape painter and etcher, or Henry Thomas (1811-1878), marine and landscape painter. Source: op.cit. C. Wood.

29. Diary, 21 January, 1879.

30. Valentine Cameron Prinsep (1838-1904). Painter of portraits, historical subjects, and genre.

31. Sir Samuel Luke Fildes (1843-1927), painter of genre and portraits.

Appendix 1

The 'Pall Mall Gazette' No.6593, Vol.XLII, 4 May, 1886, p.11.

THE "PALL MALL GAZETTE" £25 PRIZE COMPETITION.

"EVERY MAN HIS OWN ART CRITIC."

WHAT are the best pictures in the Academy? That is the question which is always asked on all sides wherever two or three are gathered together during the summer season. There is much talk "about it and about," but the world is no nearer an authoritative answer at the end than at the beginning. The Academy, which ought to be the final judge on such a question, puts itself out of court by conceding to its own members places to which they are notoriously not entitled on their merits. The oracle of Brantwood is dumb, and where is one to turn for a voice which speaks with authority and not as the scribes? What, then, is to be done? Well, do we not live in democratic days? If the popular voice may be trusted to decide the fate of empires, may it not properly be listened to on the merits of pictures? We believe it may, and to make the popular voice articulate on the question is the object of the "Pall Mall Prize Competition." We shall be met, we know, with the objection that there are absolute canons of right and wrong in art, and that the man in the street is not qualified either to find them or to apply them. Be it so. The popular verdict may turn out to be mistaken in pictures, just as it may in politics ; but is not the unprejudiced voice of the public at least as likely to go right as the personal predilection of artistic coteries? Perhaps the world may not like best what it ought to like best : but it is at any rate of great importance to ascertain what as a matter of fact it does prefer. The case is like that of the Best Books. It is highly interesting to know what books the literary lights think best worth reading ; but it is very important also to know what books are as a matter of fact most read.

What, then, are the best pictures in the Academy? Let every reader of this paper (and of every other paper—metropolitan and provincial) buy our Guide to "the Pictures of 1886," which is published to-day, become his own art critic, and fill in, according to his own opinion, the form which he will there find, and of which the following is a reduced facsimile :—

1. The Best Picture of all	
2. The Best Historical Picture	
3. The Best Landscape	
4. The Best Marine Picture	
5. The Best Animal Picture	
6. The Best Portrait	
7. The Best Domestic Picture	
8. The Best Classical Picture	
9. The Best Religious Picture	
10. The Best Water Colour Drawing ...	
11. The Prettiest Baby........................	
12. The Worst Picture........................	

The coupons—supplied only in copies of "Pictures of 1886"—must be torn out and sent to the Academy Editor, *Pall Mall Gazette*, Northumberland-street, Strand, on or before July 31, 1886. We shall then tabulate all the results, and the best pictures under the several heads will be those for which most readers have voted. In connection with this competition two prizes are offered :—First prize, £20 ; second prize, £5. The *FIRST PRIZE* will be awarded to the competitor whose list of favourites agrees most closely with the list of best pictures tabulated from the votes of all competitors. Should there be a dead heat between two or more competitors, the prize will be divided equally among them. Similarly with the *Second Prize.* It will be awarded to the competitor whose list comes second nearest to the final result, and should two or more competitors stand on an equality in this respect it will be divided equally among them. The result of the competition will be announced in the *Pall Mall Gazette* on as early a day as possible after July 31, 1886. In this manner we hope, with the co-operation of our readers, to be able for the first time to authoritatively decide what in the opinion of all intelligent people are the Best Pictures in the Academy.

It may be convenient to briefly recapitulate the three conditions of the competition :—

1. All lists must be written on the coupons supplied in copies of "Pictures of 1886."

2. All lists must be sent to the "Academy Editor," *Pall Mall Gazette*, Northumberland-street, Strand, on or before July 31, 1886.

3. Competitors must deal with pictures in the ACADEMY only.

Appendix 2

The 'Pall Mall Gazette' No.6682, Vol.XLIV, 16 August, 1886, p.2.

Results of the 'Pall Mall Gazette' competition.
Breakdown of results of 'Best Landscape'.

Leader	'With Verdure Clad'	378
Leader	'The End of the Day'	326
Cole	'Sultry Hour'	224
Cole	'Great Marlow on Thames'	148
Cole	'Pangbourne'	141
MacWirther	'The Three Witches'	114
Cole	'Cookham'	76
Johnson	'In the Midlands; Cub Hunting'	71
Brett	'An Argyll Eden'	61
MacBeth	'A Fen Lode'	48
Murray	'A Picardy Pastoral'	36
Leader	'When the West with Evening Glows'	31
Graham	'Across the Moor'	28
East	'By Tranquil Waters'	25
Halswells	'The Heart of the Coolins, Isle of Skye'	20
Davis	'A Flood on the Wye'	19
Walker	'Autumn; The Thames at Cliveden'	15
Parsons	'On Shannon Shore'	14
Walton	'Waiting to the West Wind Blows'	9
Farquharson	'And Winter's Breath came Cold and Chill'	9
Wyllie	'The Estuary on the Thames'	8
Wyllie	'Work-a-Day England'	6
Macbeth	'Sodden Fen'	6

Appendix 3

Selective list of private collectors of B.W. Leader's paintings during the artist's lifetime

NAME	STATUS	TITLES AND DATES OF PAINTINGS PURCHASED
Allcroft, John Derby 1822-1893 Stokesay Court, Shropshire	Glove Manufacturer & Merchant MP Worcester	'Wetterhorn from above Rosenlaui', RA 1875, No.315. 76 x 61in (193 x 155cm). 'Stokesay Castle', 1876. 14 x 18in (35.5 x 46cm).
Ashcombe, Lord 1828-1917	1st. Baron, Surrey. Of the Cubitt family of builders who made a fortune constructing large parts of London; including – King's Cross Station and Belgravia	'Bodmin Castle', (a pair), 1894. 18 x 30in (46 x 76cm).
Armitage, Benjamin 1823-1900 Chomlea, Pendleton	Chairman of Sir Elkanah Armitage & Sons, Textile Manufacturers. Justice of the Peace. MP for Salford 1880-86	'Wild Wales', RA 1872, No.408. 60 x 72in (152.5 x 183cm). 'A Trout Stream: An Autumn Afternoon on the Llugwy', 1872. 20 x 30in (51 x 76cm). 'Tintern Abbey: Moonlight', 1872-1890. 20 x 30in (51 x 76cm).
Armitage, Samuel 1826-1906 Chaseley House, Pendleton	Director of Sir Elkanah Armitage & Sons, Textile Manufacturers	'In the Evening there shall be light', 1882-3. Study for 1882 RA picture. 48 x 72in (122 x 183cm).
Bacon, Judge (d.1911)		'Near Harlech, North Wales', 1889. 25 x 41½in (63.5 x 105.5cm).
Barran, Sir J.	Member of Parliament	'Glebe Farm on the Welsh Border', 1884, RA 1884, No.6. 50 x 74in (127 x 188cm).
Bass, Sir William (d.1925)	Brewer, Burton-upon-Trent (Founded by M.T. Bass 1799-1884)	'On the Avon Near Bristol', 1875, 41 x 70in (104 x 178cm). Until 1913
Beecham, Sir Joseph (d.1916)	Of the family of Beecham Pills fame	'A Welsh River; The River Llugwy, Bettws-y-coed', 1904, RA 1904, No.559. 36 x 56in (91.5 x 142cm).
Cartwright	Tin Toy Manufacturer, Wolverhampton	'Old Mill, Worcestershire', 1850. 11 x 14½in (28 x 37cm).
Castellian, Alfred	(F.Huth & Co.) Commissioners & General Merchants, Liverpool	'Autumn's Last Gleam', 1865, RA 1865, No.317. Paris 1867, No.80. 36 x 60in (91.5 x 152.5cm). 'A Sunny Autumn Afternoon, N. Wales', 1865, RA 1865. No.468. 30 x 52in (76 x 132cm).
Collier, Sir Arthur Robert 1817-1886 (Lord Monkwell from 1885)	Attorney General – Privy Council Judge	'At Rosenlaui', finished study, 1873. 16 x 24in (41 x 61cm). 'Goring Church', finished study, 1873. 16 x 24in (41 x 61cm).
Colman, Sir Jeremiah 1830-1924	Mustard and Starch Manufacturer	'Our South Coast', 1901, RA 1901, No.458. 48 x 72in (122 x 183cm). 'Cambria's Coast', 1889, RA 1889, No.480. (bt. 1918). 43 x 72in (109 x 183cm).
Craig, R. Hunter 1839-1937	Chairman and Founder of R.Hunter, Craig, & Co.; Flour Produce Importers. London, Liverpool and Glasgow.	'Summer Evening', 1859? Size?

NAME	STATUS	TITLES AND DATES OF PAINTINGS PURCHASED
Craigmyle, Lord. 1850-1937	Advocate. From 1905 Lord Advocate of Scotland	'Still Evening – Goring', 1884. 48 x 72in (122 x 183cm).
Crowther, Frank. Gemmil. 1835?-1905	JP for Lancaster. Head of T. & C. Littlewood and Co., Woollen Manufacturers. Also Director of Manchester, Liverpool District Banking Co.	'Glyder Fawr', 1881, RA 1881, No.521. 48 x 72in (122 x 183cm).
Dent, John	Glove Manufacturer	'The Dawn of an Autumn Day', 1889, RA 1889, No.662. 48 x 72in (122 x 183cm).
Dixon, Joshua 1811-1885	Deputy Chairman of the London, Chatham and Dover Railway Co. 1867-1870. Bequested all his art collection to the Bethnal Green Museum.	'Mill on the Llugwy', 1875, 47 x 71in (119.5 x 180.5cm).
Egerton, Lord 1832-1909	Chairman of the Manchester Ship Canal 1891-1894	'The Construction of the Manchester Ship Canal', 1891, RA 1891, No.590. 53¾ x 88in (136.5 x 223.5cm).
Faber, The Rt. Hon. Lord		'Sandbanks on the South Coast', 1905. 30 x 48in (76 x 122cm).
Gassiot, Charles	Port and Sherry Importer	'A Welsh Churchyard', 1863, RA 1863, No.440 (bt. 1875). 32 x 58in (81.5 x 147.5cm).
Gladstone, W.E. 1809-1898	Chancellor of The Exchequer. Four times Prime Minister	'A Welsh Churchyard', 1863, RA 1863, No.440 (bt. 1863). 32 x 58in (81.5 x 147.5cm).
Grant, Baron Albert. 1831-1899 (Albert Gottheimer)	Financier and property promoter of such companies as The Cadiz Waterworks and The Central Uruguayan Railways. Sale of his Art Collection 1877 because of bankruptcy	'Mountain Solitude', 1873, RA 1873, No.379. 36 x 59in (91.5 x 150cm). 'English Cottage Homes', 1873, RA 1873, No.110. 36 x 54in (91.5 x 137cm). 'Bright Autumn Night: Goring-on-Thames'. 1873, RA 1873, No.398. 36 x 59in (91.5 x 150cm).
Goldsmid Bart, Sir Julian	PC, MP	'On the Wye', 1887. 17 x 26in (43 x 66cm).
Hall, Samuel Carter. 1800-1890	Editor; Art Union Monthly Journal. Renamed The Art Journal in 1849	'Sheep Pastures', (bt. 1874). 16 x 24in (41 x 61cm). 'Thames at Goring', Autumn 1874. 14 x 18in (35.5 x 46cm).
Harding, Sir R.P. 1821-1893	Accountant	'A Worcestershire Cottage', 1864. 19 x 26in (48.5 x 66cm).
Hargreaves, Col. John		'Ploughman Homeward Plods...', 1884. 26 x 44in (66 x 112cm).
Heape, Robert Taylor 1848-1904 Rochdale, Lancs.	Flannel Manufacturer	'Haymaking', 1881, (bt. 1904). 16 x 24in (41 x 61cm).
Hindlip, Lord. (Charles Alsopp)	JP & DC for Worcestershire	'View from Doveridge Hall', 1889?
Holcroft, William	Rufford Fire Clay Works, Stourbridge	'The Wellhorn from Rosenlaui', RA 1873, No.974. 57½ x 39in (146 x 99cm). 'A Welsh Hillside Path', 1874. RA 1874, No.657. 41 x 58in (104 x 147.5cm).
Holloway, Thomas	Financied the building of the Royal Holloway College. Opened by Queen Victoria 1886 (Made fortune from pills and ointments)	'A Rocky Bed of a Welsh River', 1874, (bt. after 1901). 48 x 36in (122 x 91.5cm).

NAME	STATUS	TITLES AND DATES OF PAINTINGS PURCHASED
Ingram, Herbert 1811–1860	Founder of the *Illustrated London News*	'The Warren Gate', 1859? 'Early Summer Time', 1859? 'A Beech Wood', 1889. 18 x 26in (45.5 x 66cm).
Ingram, Sir William 1847–1924	MD of the *Illustrated London News* and *The Sketch* Ltd.	'On the Avon, near Bristol', 1875, (bt. c.1913). 41 x 70in (104 x 178cm). 'Sandy Margins of the Sea', 1890, RA 1890, No.131. 48 x 71¾in (122 x 182.5cm).
Joicey, James 1st. Lord Joicey of Chester le Street, Durham	Coal Mine Owner	'Willy Lot's House: The Subject of Constable', 1901. 12 x 18in (30.5 x 46cm). 'Old Cottage, Whittington', 1902. 36 x 30in (91.5 x 76cm).
Kelk, Sir John		'The Wetterhorn from above Rosenlaui', 1873. 52 x 72in (132 x 183cm).
Lever, Lord W.H. (d.1925)	Port Sunlight Fame	'Worcester Cathedral', 1894, RA 1894, No.371, (bt. 1913). 54 x 90in (137 x 229cm). 'Evening - Worcestershire', signed & dated ? (bt. c.1913).
Littlewood, John Stothert 1838–1918 Headly Hall, Rochdale	Flannel Manufacturer	'Scene on the Llugwy, Moel Siabod in the Distance', 1870. 16 x 24in (41 x 61cm).
Loughlin, Martin, Australia	One of the founding members of the City of Ballararat Art Gallery	'The Village Inn', 1889. 32 x 48in (81.5 x 122cm).
Lovatt, Henry Wolverhampton	Builder	'An English River in Autumn', 1877. 24 x 36in (61 x 91.5cm). 'The Valley of the Llugwy', 1883. 24 x 36in (61 x 91.5cm).
Lycett, Sir Frank		'The Farm, Whittington', 1862. 'Church & River, Bettws-y-coed', 1864-96. 31 x 51in (79 x 129.5cm). 'Figures in a Hayfield', 1868.
MacDonald, Alexander jun., d.1884 Perthshire	Inherited father's wealth and granite industry	Self-Portrait by B.W.Leader, 1884. 14 x 12in (35.5 x 30.5cm).
Maharajah of Lahore, India		'Sunshine after a Shower', 1887, RA 1887, No.52. 41 x 60in (104 x 152.5cm).
Mappin, Sir Frederick Thorpe (nephew of J.N. Mappin)	MP	'The Lledr Bridge near Bettws-y-coed', 1865. 18 x 26in (46 x 66cm).
Mappin, John Newton 1800–1883	Sheffield Industrialist: Brewery Business	'A Flood on a Welsh River', 1872, RA, No.151. 35 x 53in (89 x 135cm).
Mather, William Salford	MP. Father owned Salford Iron Works	'Wild Wales', 1872, RA 1872, No.408. (bt. May 1900). 60 x 72in (152.5 x 183cm).
McCulloch, George d.1907	Australian Millionaire. President, Chairman or Director of several international mining companies.	'By Mead and Stream', 1893, RA 1893, No.499. RA Loan Exhib. 1909, No.71. 53 x 89in (135 x 226cm). 'Worcester Cathedral', 1894, RA 1894, No.371. RA Loan Exhibition, 1909, No.127. 54 x 90in (137 x 228.5cm). 'When Sun is Set', 1892, Chicago 1893. RA Loan Exhibition, 1909, No.130. 44 x 72in (111.5 x 183cm). 'Conway Bay and Carnarvonshire Coast', 1892, RA 1892, No.417, Chicago 1893, RA Loan Exhibition, 1909, No.222. 52 x 84in (132 x 213.5cm).

NAME	STATUS	TITLES AND DATES OF PAINTINGS PURCHASED
Mount-Stephens, Lord 1833–1911	Canada B.C. & Co., Banff	'Wye at Tintern, Moonlight', 1872. 30 x 50in (76 x 127cm). 'On the Teme', 1883. 12 x 18in (30.5 x 46cm).
Napier, Montague Stanley 1870–1931	Car Manufacturer & Aero-engine designer	'Sands of Aberdovey', 1888, RA 1888, No.421. 44 x 72in (112 x 183cm).
Overtoun, Lord		'Sunset: A Golden Eve', 1896, RA 1896, No.184. 48 x 72in (122 x 183cm). 'A Silvery Morn', 1896, RA 1896, No.617. 48 x 72in (122 x 183cm).
Palmer, G.E.	MP	'Parting Day', 1883, finished study of the 1883 RA picture, No.98. 25 x 41½in (63.5 x 105.5cm). 'Birch Clad Hill and Shallow Stream', 1903, RA 1903, No.502. 36 x 56in (91.5 x 142cm).
Palmer, William Isaac	Partner: Huntley & Palmer Biscuits	'A Mill on the Machno, North Wales', 1862. 13½ x 11½in (34 x 30cm).
Patterson, Pattison, R. (d.1899)	Distiller. Leith and Edinburgh	'A Path through a Surrey Wood', 1897. 13 x 18in (33 x 46cm). 'A Surrey Lane', 1897. 13 x 17in (33 x 43cm).
Pender, Sir John 1813–1896	Pioneer of Sub-Marine Telegraphy	'In the evening there shall be light', 1882, RA 1882, No.737, Paris 1889, No.83. 45 x 72in (114.5 x 183cm).
Perrins, J. Dyson	Lea & Perrins Worcs. Sauce fame Director, Royal Worcester Porcelain Factory	'Wild Water', 1875, RA 1875, No.554. 35 x 52in (89 x 132cm).
Portman, Viscount		'Smooth Severn Stream', 1887, RA 1887, No.496 (bt.1894). 36 x 64in (91.5 x 162.5cm).
Price, David 1809–1891	Wool Merchant; Messrs Price & Co., 16 Gresham Street, London Art Patron; private gallery, Queen Anne Street	'Knightsford Bridge', signed & dated ? (bt.1872). 'Mountain Solitude', 1875. 16 x 24in (41 x 61cm). 'Meeting of the Conway and the Llugwy', 1866. 15 x 24in (38 x 61cm).
Quilter, Sir William Cuthbert 1841–1911	One of the founders of The National Telephone Co.	'Green Pastures and Still Waters', 1883, RA, No.508. 48 x 72in (122 x 183cm). 'Parting Day', 1883, RA 1883, No.98. 48 x 72in (122 x 183cm).
Reckitt, Sir James 1833–1924	Starch Manufacturer	'Dewy Morning on the Mountains, Capel Curig, N. Wales', 1874, RA 1874, No.505 (bt after 1887). 49 x 71in (124.5 x 180.5cm).
Reiss, Emil Salford	General Merchant	'Church and Lock, Stratford-on-Avon', 1883. 55 x 41in (140 x 104cm). 'On the Coast, Llandrilas, N. Wales', 1888. 6 x 9in (15 x 23cm).
Russell-Cotes, Sir Merton 1835–1921	Hotelier in Bournemouth	'Lledr Valley', 1866-94. 28 x 40½in (71 x 103cm). 'Head of Derwent Water, Sunset', 1870-77. 27 x 45in (68.5 x 114.5cm). 'A Welsh River', 1907, RA 1907, No.157. 36 x 56in (91.5 x 142cm).
Shaw, R.	MP	'Flood on the Llugwy', 1871. 14 x 18in (35.5 x 46cm).
Stanley, William Ford Robinson 1829–1909	Manufacturer of Scientific Instruments Local benefactor, Croydon, Surrey	'St. Michael's Mount', 1877. (bt. c.1890). 36 x 54in (91.5 x 137cm).
Starkie, Colonel	Army	'Old Holyhead Road', 1885, RA 1885, No.1033. 49 x 84in (124.5 x 213.5cm).

NAME	STATUS	TITLES AND DATES OF PAINTINGS PURCHASED
Tate, Sir Henry 1819-1899	Head of Henry Tate and Sons, Sugar Refineries Liverpool and London	'Valley of the Llugwy', 1883. 47 x 79in (119.5 x 201cm).
Vassar-Smith, Sir Richard	Clearing Banker (Chairman, Lloyds Bank 1909-1922)	'On Dartmoor', 1876. 17 x 36in (43 x 91.5cm). 'Scene on a Welsh River', 1877. 14 x 18in (35.5 x 46cm).
Virtue, James S.	Publisher, *The Art Journal*	'Tintern Abbey by Moonlight', 1873. 16 x 24in (41 x 61cm). 'Island on the Llugwy', 1875. 25 x 43in (63.5 x 109cm).
Walker, Thomas (d.1887) Birmingham	Manufacturer. The Patent Shaft and Axle Co.	'Goring Church', 1874. 20 x 30in (51 x 76cm). 'Thames near Pangbourne', 1874. 16 x 24in (41 x 61cm). 'The Rocky Bed of a Welsh river', 1874. 48 x 36in (122 x 91.5cm). 'A Quiet Nook near Capel Curig', 1875. 16 x 24in (41 x 61cm).
Werthiemer, A.	*Graphic Magazine*	'On the Carnarvon Coast', 1892. 20 x 30in? (51 x 76cm?).
White, Sir George (Bt.) 1854-1916	Tramway promoter and aeroplane manufacturer Bristol	'Bernards Green', 1900. 24 x 36in (61 x 91.5cm). 'Worcestershire Hayfield', 1901. 20 x 30in (51 x 76cm). 'Thames at Streatley', 1903. 16 x 24in (41 x 61cm).
Wilson, John Edmund 1884?-1907 Birmingham	Head of Albright and Wilson, the first major British firm manufacturing commercial chemicals	'February Fill Dyke', 1881, RA 1881, No.42, Manchester Jubilee Exhib. 1887, No.23. 47 x 72in (119.5 x 183cm).
Woodiwiss, George	Mayor of Bath 1896 Founder of the Victoria Art Gallery, Bath	'A Quiet Evening', 1892. 24 x 40in (41 x 102cm).
Yates, John E.	The largest Cotton Spinner in Rochdale	'Shere Church', 1892. 30 x 48in (76 x 122cm). 'At evening time it shall be light', 1897. 30 x 50in (76 x 127cm).

SOURCES: Leader's Diaries and Sales Records; Agnews' Stock Books; Christie's and Sotheby's Catalogues. Biographical information has been drawn from various sources including *The Dictionary of National Biography*, *Who Was Who*, the local and national press, *Salter's* and Trade Directories.

Appendix 4

Exhibited Paintings at the Royal Academy
(Measurements, where shown, are height by width).

B. Williams, Diglis House, Worcester.

1854	184	Cottage Children Blowing Bubbles	Size unknown
1855	110	The Bird Trap	Size unknown
	1357	Evening, Return to the Homestead	Size unknown
1856	718	The Young Mother. 'Lo! at the couch where infant beauty sleeps, etc.' – Campbell 'Pleasures of Hope'	18 x 24in (46 x 61cm)

B. Leader, Diglis House, Worcester.

1857	268	A Stream from the Hills	Size unknown (small)
	592	An English Homestead	27 x 35½in (68.5 x 90cm)
1858		Pictures accepted but not hung	

B.W. Leader, Diglis House, Worcester.

1859	10	The Heath from Albury	17½ x 25½in (44.5 x 65cm)
1859	559	A Sketch on a Common	Size unknown
	922	A Chat by the Way	18 x 14in? (46 x 35.5cm)
	933	A Quiet Pool in Glen Falloch	Size unknown
1860	344	Evening; North Wales	Size unknown
	467	A Quiet Valley amongst the Welsh Hills	28 x 42¾in (71 x 108.5cm)
	507	A Worcestershire Lane	Size unknown

B.W. Leader, 3 Serjeant's Inn, London.

1861	539	Still Evening	42 x 61in (107 x 155cm)
1862	369	An Autumn Afternoon, Worcestershire	Size unknown
	484	Summertime	Size unknown

B.W. Leader, Whittington, Worcester.

1863	440	A Welsh Churchyard	32 x 58in (81.5 x 147.5cm)
1864	316	An English Country Churchyard, Autumn	32 x 53in (81.5 x 135cm)
	575	A Sunny Afternoon, North Wales	35½ x 43½in (68.5 x 90cm)
1865	317	Autumn's Last Gleam. 'When yellow leaves, or none or few do hang upon these boughs, etc.'	36 x 60in (91.5 x 152.5cm)
	468	A Sunny Autumn Afternoon, North Wales	29½ x 52½in (75 x 133.5cm)

B.W. Leader, The Lodge, Whittington.

1866	182	The Close of Summer	36 x 60in (91.5 x 152.5cm)
	573	A Fine Day in Autumn, North Wales	28¾ x 51in (73 x 129.5cm)
1867	501	An Autumn Evening in the Valley of the Lledr	40 x 65in (101.5 x 165cm)
	528	Through the Glen	34 x 52in (86.5 x 132cm)
1868	113	A Fine Morning in Early Spring	27 x 48in (69 x 122cm)
	128	A Moated Grange	28½ x 42in (72.5 x 107cm)
1869	63	An English Riverside Cottage	Size unknown
	201	Looking down a Welsh River	Size unknown
1870	167	Chepstow Castle	30 x 52in (76 x 132cm)
	979	The Lock and Church, Stratford-on-Avon	35 x 54in (89 x 137cm)
1871	591	The Stream through the Birchwood	40 x 60in (102 x 152.5cm)
	1122	An Autumn Evening	40 x 58in (102 x 147.5cm)
1872	130	Passing Clouds Near Capel Curig, North Wales	35½ x 55in (90 x 140cm)
	151	A Flood on a Welsh River	35 x 53in (89 x 135cm)
	408	Wild Wales	60 x 72in (152.5 x 183cm)
1873	110	English Cottage Homes	36 x 54in (91.5 x 137cm)
	379	Mountain Solitude	36 x 59in (91.5 x 150cm)
	398	A Bright Night; Goring on Thames	36 x 59in (91.5 x 150cm)
	974	The Wellhorn from Rosenlaui	57½ x 39½in (146 x 100.5cm)

1874	505	A Dewy Morning on the Mountains; Capel Curig, North Wales	49 x 71in (124.5 x 180.5cm)
	563	A Fine Day in Autumn; The Thames at Streatley	24 x 36in (61 x 91.5cm)
	657	A Welsh Hillside Path	41 x 58in (104 x 147.5cm)
1875	315	The Wetterhorn from above Rosenlaui	76 x 61in (193 x 155cm)
	554	Wild Water	35 x 52in (89 x 132cm)
1876	20	An Autumn Evening; Barges passing a Lock on the Thames	48 x 72in (122 x 183cm)
	202	A November Evening; Clearing up after Rain	Size unknown
	441	An English Hayfield	Size unknown
1877	508	A Fine Autumn Night; Lucerne	Size unknown
	1348	In the Valley of Clear Springs; Lauterbrunnen	48 x 72in (122 x 183cm)
1878	122	Autumn in Switzerland; on the road from Meyringen to Rosenlaui	52 x 72in (132 x 183cm)
	135	Summer Time in Worcestershire	36 x 72in (91.5 x 183cm)
1879	50	An English Hayfield	35½ x 54in (90 x 137cm)
	964	The Last Gleam	37 x 59in (94 x 150cm)
1880	1480	A Gleam in the Storm	47 x 71in (119.5 x 180.5cm)
	1505	A Summer Flood; North Wales	35½ x 53½in (90 x 136cm)
1881	42	February Fill Dyke	47 x 71½in (119.5 x 182cm)
	521	Glyder Fawr	48 x 72in (122 x 183cm)
1882	550	Morning; the Banks of the Ivy O	Size unknown (? x 72?)
	737	'In the evening there shall be light'	45 x 72in (114.5 x 183cm)

Elected Associate of the Royal Academy

1883	98	Parting Day. 'The weary sun hath made a golden set, And, by the bright track of his fiery car, Gives token of a goodly day tomorrow'	48 x 72in (122 x 183cm)
	508	Green Pastures and Still Waters	48 x 72in (122 x 183cm)
	1471	An Autumn Evening	Size unknown (? x 72?)
1884	6	A Glebe Farm on the Welsh Border	50 x 74in (127 x 188cm)
	130	'Flow down, cold rivulet, to the sea, thy tribute wave deliver'	Size unknown 24 x 36in? (61 x 91.5cm)
	902	'The ploughman homeward plods his weary way'	47 x 83in (119.5 x 211cm)
1885	254	A Worcestershire Lane after a Summer Shower	42 x 32½in (107 x 82.5cm)
	555	'Hedgerow elms on hillocks green'	47½ x 71½in (121 x 182cm
	1033	The Old Holyhead Road through North Wales	49 x 84in (124.5 x 213.5cm)
1886	346	'When the west with evening glows'	36 x 60in (91.5 x 152.5cm)
	654	The End of the Day	48 x 72in (122 x 183cm)
	964	'With Verdure Clad'	42 x 87in (107 x 221cm)
1887	52	Sunset after a Shower	41 x 60in (104 x 152.5cm)
	496	'Smooth Severn Stream' – Milton	36 x 64in (91.5 x 162.5cm)
	512	A Sheepfold	35 x 59in (89 x 150cm)
	682	An April Day; 'Sweet day, so cool, so calm, so bright, etc.' – Herbert	50 x 84in (127 x 213.5cm)
1888	408	An Old English Homestead	48 x 72in (122 x 183cm)
	421	The Sands of Aberdovey	44 x 72in (111.5 x 183cm)
	638	A Summer's Day. 'When the south wind congregates in crowds. The floating mountains of the silver clouds'	52 x 84in (132 x 213.5cm)
1889	480	Cambria's Coast	43 x 72in (109 x 183cm)
	654	Sabrina's Stream	48 x 72in (122 x 183cm)
	662	The Dawn of an Autumn Day	48 x 72in (122 x 183cm)
	1162	The Incoming Tide	Size unknown

B.W. Leader, Burrows Cross, Gomshall

1890	131	The Sandy Margins of the Sea	48 x 72in (122 x 183cm)
	458	Where Sea and River Meet	45 x 72in (114.5 x 183cm)
	672	The Silent Evening Hour	56 x 84in (142 x 213.5cm)
1891	482	Solitude	59 x 47in (150 x 119.5cm)
	690	Construction of the Manchester Ship Canal	53¾ x 88in (136.5 x 223.5cm)
	982	Sand-Dunes	45 x 69in (114.5 x 175.5cm)
	1130	Still Evening	Size unknown (? x 60in?)
1892	167	Across the Common	43½ x 71in (110.5 x 180.5cm)
	417	Conway Bay and the Carnarvonshire Coast	52 x 84in (132 x 213.5cm)
	634	A Surrey Sandpit	36 x 57in (91.5 x 145cm)

1893	3	A Hillside Road	48 x 72in (122 x 183cm)
	39	Carting Timber	36 x 56in (91.5 x 142cm)
	252	An Old Country Churchyard 'With ivy mantle clad'	48 x 72in (122 x 183cm)
	499	By Mead and Stream	53 x 89in (135 x 226cm)
1894	164	A Wet Roadside	47 x 72in (119.5 x 183cm)
	317	A Surrey Woodland	30 x 48in (76 x 122cm)
	371	Worcester Cathedral	54 x 90in (137 x 228.5cm)
	484	A Village Church	48 x 72in (122 x 183cm)
1895	43	Evening	Size unknown
	392	English Cottage Homes	44 x 72in (112 x 183cm)
	481	A Sunny Morning – Surrey	60 x 48in (152.5 x 122cm)
	534	Evening Glow	50 x 84in (127 x 213.5cm)
1896	184	A Golden Eve	48 x 72in (122 x 183cm)
	448	The Skirts of a Pine Wood	72 x 48in (183 x 122cm)
	617	A Silvery Morn	48 x 72in (122 x 183cm)
	837	Hill-Side Pines	24 x 20in (61 x 51cm)
1897	268	The Breezy Morn	48 x 72in (122 x 183cm)
	398	'Fast falls the eventide'	44 x 71in (112 x 180.5cm)
	554	An Autumn Gleam	Size unknown (? x 60in?)
	913	On a Surrey Common	Size unknown

Elected Royal Academician.

1898	188	In a Welsh Valley	48½ x 72in (123 x 183cm)
	309	'Where peaceful waters glide'	43½ x 72in (110.5 x 183cm)
	314	The Silver Sea	Size unknown (44 x 72in?)
	952	Surrey Sheep Pastures	36 x 60in (91.5 x 152.5cm)
1899	23	The Sand-pit – Burrows Cross (Diploma Work)	24 x 40in (61 x 101.5cm)
	183	Evening's Last Gleam	46 x 72in (117 x 183cm)
	355	'Where brook and river meet'	Size unknown (48 x 72in?)
	508	'Summer eve by haunted stream'	48 x 72in (122 x 183cm)
1900	175	Hill, Vale and Stream	44 x 72in (112 x 183cm)
	249	When Sun is Set	36 x 60in (91.5 x 152.5cm)
	376	'At the close of day, when the hamlet is still'	44 x 72in (112 x 183cm)
	839	A Trout Stream	Size unknown
1901	175	A Gleam before the Storm	Size unknown (48 x 72in?)
	445	An Old Southern Port	44 x 72in (112 x 183cm)
	458	Our South Coast	48 x 72in (122 x 183cm)
	810	The Weald of Surrey	60 x 48in (152.5 x 122cm)
1902	152	Across the Heath	48 x 72in (122 x 183cm)
	270	The Way to the Village Church	Size unknown (48 x 72in?)
	483	Evening Light	60 x 48in (152.5 x 122cm)
	745	An Old Manor House 'For over all there hung a cloud of fear, etc.'	36 x 60in (91.5 x 152.5cm)
1903	12	'Southward from Surrey's pleasant hills'	60½ x 48½ in (154 x 123cm)
	191	Sunset after Rain	48 x 72in (122 x 183cm)
	443	A Coming Storm	36 x 48in (91.5 x 122cm)
	502	A Birch-Clad Hill and Shallow Stream	36½ x 56in (93 x 142cm)
1904	14	A Sandy Shore on the South Coast	36 x 64in (91.5 x 162.5cm)
	168	A Quiet Evening	48 x 71in (122 x 180.5cm)
	184	Evening among the Surrey Pines	36 x 58in (91.5 x 147.5cm)
	559	A Welsh River	36½ x 56½in (93 x 143.5cm)
1905	79	Sunshine and Showers on the South Coast	36 x 56in (91.5 x 142cm)
	172	The Silvery Thames	Size unknown
	427	The Evening Hour	60 x 48in (152.5 x 122cm)
	485	The Incoming Tide on the Cornish Coast	43½ x 71¾in 110.5 x 182cm)
1906	36	Evening Glow	36 x 56in (91.5 x 142cm)
	50	A Grey Day on a Flowery Stream	24 x 36in (61 x 91.5cm)
	211	The Wooded Banks of the Thames at Shillingford	32 x 60in (81.5 x 152.5cm)
	803	A Summer's Day on the Thames	35 x 60in (89 x 152.5cm)
1907	52	Evening	48 x 72in (122 x 183cm)
	157	A Welsh River	36 x 56in (91.5 x 142cm)
	182	A Shallow Stream at Eventide	48 x 72in (122 x 183cm)
	652	A Circus by the Sea	Size unknown
1908	171	A Summer's Morn, North Wales	48 x 72in (122 x 183cm)
	294	On the Golf Links, Littlehampton	Size unknown
	366	Sunset on the Surrey Wolds	36 x 60in (91.5 x 152.5cm)

TITLE	ENGRAVER/ ETCHER	STYLE	SIZE	STATES	NO.	PRICE(£)	YEAR PUBLISHED & PUBLISHER
'A Breezy Day' (After the 1897 RA Pict., No.268)	Th. Chauvel	Etching	18 x 27½in (46 x 70cm)	A.P. Vellum Present. Prints	350 25	10.10.0 2.2.0	11 Sept. 1899 A. Tooth & Sons
'The Silent Restfulness of Eve' (Poss. after the 1898 Pict. of the same title)	C. Fonce	Etching	17 x 27¾in (43 x 70.5cm)	A.P. Present. Prints	300 25	8.8.0 2.2.0	2 May 1899 I.P. Mendoza
'The Toils of the Day are Over' Exhib'd. RA 1899, No.1583. (After the 1897 Pict. of same title)	David Law R.E.	Etching	13⅝ x 20⅝ in (34.5 x 52cm)	A.P. signed by Artist & Etcher	400	5.5.0	1899 J.S. Virtue & Co. Ltd.
'The Rocky Bed of a Welsh River' Exhib'd. RA 1899, No.1441. (After the 1874 Pict. of same title)	David Law R.E.	Etching	20 x 14½in (51 x 37cm)	A.P. signed by Artist & Etcher	400	5.5.0	1899 J.S. Virtue & Co. Ltd.
'Summer Eve by Haunted Stream' (After the 1899 RA Pict., No.508)	C. Fonce	Etching	19 x 28⅛in (48.5 x 71cm)	A.P. Present. Prints	250 25	8.8.0 2.2.0	12 Oct. 1900 I.P. Mendoza
'Fast falls the eventide' (After the 1897 RA Pict., No.398)	Th. Chauvel	Etching	17⅛ x 28⅛in (43 x 71cm)	A.P. Vellum Present. Prints	350 25	10.10.0 2.2.0	24 Apr. 1900 A. Tooth & Sons
'In a Welsh Valley' (After the 1898 RA Pict., No.188)	Th. Chauvel	Etching	19 x 28¾in (48.5 x 73cm)	A.P. Vellum Present. Prints	350 25	10.10.0 2.2.0	1 July 1902 A. Tooth & Sons
'The Ploughman Homeward Plods his Weary Way' (After the 1884 Pict. of same title)	Henry Scott Bridgwater	Mezzo-tint	14¼ x 24¼in (36 x 62cm)	A.P. Present. Prints	300 25	6.6.0 1.1.0	12 Aug. 1902 Leggatt Bros.
'The Weald of Surrey'. (After the 1901 RA Pict., No.810)	B. Debaines	Etching	25 x 20½in (63.5 x 52cm)	A.P. Present Prints	350 25	8.8.0 2.2.0	9 Sept. 1902 T. Agnew & Sons
'Evening Light'. Companion to 'Among the Surrey Pine Trees'. (After the 1902 RA Pict., No.483)	Camille Fonce	Etching	25 x 20in (63.5 x 51cm)	A.P. Present. Prints	300 25	8.8.0 1.1.0	3 Sept. 1902 H. Graves & Co., Ltd.
'Among the Surrey Pines'. Companion to 'Evening Light' (After the 1900 Pict. titled 'Evening Among the Surrey Pines')	C. Fonce	Etching	25¼ x 19⅝in (64 x 50cm)	A.P. Present. Prints	300 25	8.8.0 1.1.0	Sept. 1902 H. Graves & Co., Ltd.

TITLE	ENGRAVER/ ETCHER	STYLE	SIZE	STATES	NO.	PRICE(£)	YEAR PUBLISHED & PUBLISHER
'The Gleam before the Storm' (After the 1901 RA Pict., No.175)	A. Boulard	Etching	18¾x 28 in (48 x 71cm)	A.P. Present. Prints	350 25	10.10.0 2.2.0	28 Sept. 1902 A. Tooth & Sons
'A Surrey Sandpit' (After the 1899 RA Pict., No.23)	Th. Chauvel	Etching	13 x 20½ in (33 x 52cm)	A.P. Present. Prints	250 25	6.6.0 1.1.0	14 Feb. 1903 A. Tooth & Sons
'The Way to the Village Church' (After the 1902 RA Pict., No.270)	A. Boulard	Etching	18⅛x 27⅜in (46 x 70cm)	A.P. Present. Prints	350 25	10.10.0 2.2.0	20 May 1903 A. Tooth & Sons
'Southward from Surrey's Pleasant Hills' (After the 1903 RA Pict., No.12)	Th. Chauvel	Etching	21¾x 17⅜in (55.5 x 44.5cm)	A.P. Present. Prints	250 25	6.6.0 1.1.0	12 July 1904 A. Tooth & Sons
'Where Brook and River Meet' (After the 1899 RA Pict., No.355)	A. Boulard	Etching	18 x 27½in (46 x 70cm)	A.P.Vellum Present. Prints	350 25	10.10.0 2.2.0	June 1904 A. Tooth & Sons
'Streatley Mill' (Poss. after the 1904 Pict. of same title)	A. Boulard	Etching	14⅝x 23⅝in (37 x 60cm)	A.P. Present. Prints	250 25	8.8.0 1.1.0	19 April 1905 A. Tooth & Sons
'Early Morning: Goring on Thames'		Photo-gravure	13 x 20½ in (33 x 52cm)				1906 Artist's Photographic Co. Ltd.
'Departing Day at Tintern'		Photo-gravure	13 x 20½in (33 x 52cm)				Artist's Photographic Co. Ltd.
'Wooded Banks of the Thames at Shillingford' (After the 1906 RA pict., No.211)	Th. Chauvel	Etching	12¾x 24 in (32.5 x 61cm)	A.P. Present. Prints	250 25	6.6.0 1.1.0	18 Oct. 1907 A. Tooth & Sons
'Surrey Pines' (After the 1916 RA Pict., No.374)		Photo-gravure	24⅛x 16¾in (61 x 42.5cm)	A.P. I. Prints	200	3.3.0 1.1.0	1918 Frost & Reed Ltd.
'Eventide' (After an 1893 Pict.)		Photo-gravure	17⅝x 28¾in (44.5 x 73cm)	A.P.			Berlin Photographic Co. 1894
'The Church and River at Bettws-y-coed' (After an 1864 painting)	J. & G.P. Nicolls	Engraving					J.S. Virtue & Co. Ltd. (1st publ'd. *Art Journal* Feb. 1871, p.46)
'The Birch Wood near Capel, North Wales' (Poss. after an 1867 Pict. 'A Hazy Morning in a Welsh Birch Wood')	J. & G.P. Nicolls	Engraving					J.S. Virtue & Co. Ltd. (1st publ'd. *Art Journal* Feb. 1871, p.47)

'Pall Mall Gazette', 69–70, (see Appendices 1 and 2, pp.121–122)
'Saturday Review', 23, 80
'Strand Magazine', 63, 101
'Windsor Magazine', 101
Plymouth, 46, 50, 100
Poussin, Nicolas (1593/4–1665), 36
Pre-Raphaelite,
    Artists, 8, 21, 25, 29, 57
    Brotherhood, 18
    School, 36
    Style, 18, 28, 33, 38, 61
Price, David, 39, p.116: EN 16 (also see Appendix 3)
Prints, Appendix 6, pp.132–138

Quaker
    Birth Register, 10,
    'disownment', 10, p.112: EN 4, (Background and Formative Years)
    Religious Society of Friends, 10
Quilter, Harry, 77. p.118: EN 4
Quilter, Sir William Cuthbert (1841–1911), 67

Reading (Berkshire), 10
Rivers:
    Arun, 97–98
    Avon, 43, 65, 67
    Conway, 28, 36
    Lledr, 28
    Llugwy, 28, 30, 67–68, 70
    Salwarpe, 67
    Severn, 12–14, 34, **34**, **41**, 42, 67, 74, **75**, 77, 87, 97
    Stour, 97
    Teme, 33, 67
    Thames, 33, 47–48, **48**, 67
    Wye, 45
Rochdale, 84
    Art Gallery, 26–27
Rosa, Salvator (1615–1673), 21, 36, 95
Royal Academy, 21–22, 25
    Burlington House, 24–25
    Chantry Bequest, 62
    Club, 67, 90
    Council, 23–26, 54, 62, 91, **91**, p.119: EN 1 (Sunset Years: 1899–1923)
    Diploma Work, 91–92
    Exhibition of Living Artists, 24
    General Assembly Election, 37
    Members, 62
    Old Masters Exhibitions, 59, 77, p.117: EN 39
    President, 24, 39, 42, 91
        Eastlake, Sir Charles Lock (1850–1865)
        Grant, Sir Francis (1866–1878)
        Millais, Sir John Everett, Bt. (1896)

Poynter, Sir Edward John, Bt. (1896–1918)
    Schools, 14
    Selection Committee, 23–25
    Summer Exhibitions, 8, 15, 22, 31, 37, 56, 97, 106, 108
    Trafalgar Square, 24–25
    Varnishing Days, 23, 38
    Winter Loan Exhibition, 106
Royal Collection, 101
Ruskin, John, 23, 25, 29, 36, 93
    'Modern Painters', 21
    'Academy Notes', 23
Royal Mail, 93

Sanatogen, 101
Scotland, 23, **25**, 26–27 (see also Glasgow)
Scott, Sir Walter, 93
Second World War, 106
Severn Navigational Commission, The, 13, p.113: ENs 28–30
Shakespeare, William
    Romeo and Juliet, 8
Shere, 27, 78, 84, 86
    Church, **83**, **84**, 83–84, **86**, 86–87, **87**, 109
    Lych Gate, 86, p.119: EN 37
    Parish Magazine, **87**, 90, p.119: EN 44
    'White Horse', 86
Sheriff, A.C., (MP for Worcester), 30
Shillingford, 48
Silver Street Academy, Worcester, 14
Signatures, examples of,106–107, **107**
Smith-Carington, Richard, 18, 56, 76, 90, p.118: EN 19
South Coast Railway Company, 97
Stephens, Frederick George (1828–1907), 61, 69, 70
St John's Wood, 56, 62
St Michael's Mount, **52**, 53
St Petersburg, 106
Southport Corporation, 101
Stokesay Castle, 42
Stourbridge, 33
Stourport-on-Severn, 13–14, 34, **34**
Stratford-on-Avon, 43, **43**
Streatley-on-Thames, 47–48
    Mill, **47**
Surrey, 26–27
    Abinger (Hammer), 27, 87
    Albury, 22, 32, 86
        Heath, 105
        Old Parish Church of, **84**, 86
        Park, 27, 86 (see also Drummond, Henry)
    Burrows Cross, 27, 77, **78**, **79**, 86, 105, 109
        House, 78–79, **78**, **79**, 82–83, **82–83**, 90, 93, **93**, **94**, 100, 106, 109

        Garden, 78, **78**
        Sand pit, 91–92, **92**
    Chantries Wood, 92
    Holmbury St Mary, 100
    Little London, 86
    Pitch Hill, 100
    Redstone, 27
    St Martha's Hill, 92
    Tillingbourne Stream, 84, 87
        Valley, 27
    Weald, 27
    Weston Street, 86
    Winterfold Ridge, 109
Sussex, West,
    Amberley, 97
    Arundel
        Castle, 97
        George Constable, 99
    Bury, 97
        Ferry, 97, p.120: EN 12
    Climping Windmill, 99
    Littlehampton, 97–98
        Funfair, 99, **99**
        Harbour, 98–99, **98**
        South Terrace, 97, 99, **99**
        Windmill, 99, **99**
Switzerland, 46, **46**, 53, **53**, 56, 92
    Interlaken, 53
    Lucerne, 41
    Unterseen, 53, **53**
Symon, Sir Josiah, 108

Tate, Henry, 67
Taylor, Tom, 22–23, 36, 38, 48, 55
Third Queen's Regiment, 105
Thomas, Serjeant, 33
Tilling Bourne (see Surrey)
Tintagel, 45, **45**
Tintern Abbey, 45, **44**
Topham, Alice, 100
Towyn, 70
Tringham, Lt.-Col., 100
Trinity College, Cambridge, 100
Tug'Jumna', The, 98, **98**

Underwood, Thomas, 16, 23
Unterseen, 53, **53**

Victoria, Queen, 8, 26, 91, 101
Volunteer Unit, 68, p.118 (Recognition and Success, Part 1): EN 6
Von Uhde, Fritz (1848–1911), 80
Vorticist Movement, 103–104
    Wyndham, Lewis Percy (1882–1957), 103

Wales, 7, 26–27, **29**, **32**, **35**, 38, 41, **49**, **71**, 92
    Aberdovey, 70, **70**
    Aberystwyth, 72

Betws-y-coed, 28, 36, 48
  Clogwyn Gyrau, 30
  Mynydd Garthmyn, 36
  'The Royal Oak', 28
Bryn Bethynau farm, 68
Cae Gwegi farmhouse, 28
Capel Curig
  Cyfyng Bridge, 70
  Cyfyng Falls, 68
  Tyn-y-coed Hotel, 28
Cardiganshire, 70
  Cardigan Bay, 72
Carnarvonshire, 70
Clyro (Radnorshire), 31
Dovey Junction, 72
Llyn-y-Gader, 38
Wallingford, 48
Wheeley-Lea, Charles ('Chas'.), 30
Mrs, 30
Whitchurch, 48
Whiting, Henry, 15
Whittington, 32-34, **33**, 42, 58-59, 67, 72, 77, 108-109, **109** (see also Worcestershire)
Williams, family of painters, 22, 30, p.114: EN 3
Williams,
  Benjamin Leader (1831-1923)
  Benjamin Leader, 22
  Benjamin Williams Leader, 22
  Edward Leader (1802-1879. B.W.L.'s father), 10-13, **11**, 16, 59, p.112: ENs 7 and 8, p.113: ENs 27 and 32, p.117: EN 35
    'Gillingham Mill', 12, 95, 113, p.113: EN 15
    'Recollections of Ventnor. . .', 113, p.113: EN 17
    'Sharpness Point . . .', 113, p.113: EN 17
    'Tewkesbury . . .', 113, p.113: EN 17
    'Worcester from Hallow', 12
  Sarah, née Whiting (1801-1888. B.W.L.'s mother),10, **10**, 59, 76, p.118: EN 20

Edward Leader, (1828-1910. B.W.L.'s eldest brother), 14, **59,** 59, 81, p.117: EN 36 and p.119: EN 29
Sarah Edgington 'Sally' (1829-1902. B.W.L.'s eldest sister) 18, 33, 59
Helen (1852-1918. B.W.L.'s sister), 83
Alfred (1834-1913. B.W.L.'s brother), 32
Henry (1835-1917. B.W.L.'s brother)
Theophilus (1837-1854. B.W.L.'s brother), 59
Thomas Whiting (1839-1920. B.W.L.'s brother)
Maria Patty, (1840-1894. B.W.L.'s sister),18, 41, 45, 56, **59**, 76, 87, 90
Elizabeth Leader (1841-1907. B.W.L.'s sister) p.120: EN 28
Sabrina (1843-1936)
Willmore, Arthur (1814-1888), 72
  'Sheep Pastures', (Recognition and Success, Part 1) p.118: EN 15 and Appendix 5, p.137
Wilson, John Edward, 62
Windsor, Lord, 11
Wood, Mrs Henry (1814-1887), 9, 76
  'The Channings', 76
  'Mildred Arkell', 76
Worcester (see Worcestershire)
Worcestershire, 26, 72, 92-93, 110
  Bredon, 65
  Malvern, 77, 79
  Hills, 23, 74, 76
  Stonehill Common, 65
  Stourport-on-Severn, 13-14, 34, **34**
  Upton-on-Severn, 14
Whittington, 32-34, **33**, 42, 58-59, 67, 72, 77, 108-109, **109**
  Bank House, 32
  Church, 56, 63-65
  Church Farm, 33
  Lodge, 53, **55**, 55-56, 63, 76, 78, 95, **95**, 108
Worcester,
  Athenaeum, 10, 12
  Bromwich Villa, 12

Canon's House, 18
Cathedral, 12-13, 18, 68, 74
Chamber of Commerce, 30
City and County Bank, 30
City Art Gallery, 30
Deanery, 18, 74
Diglis House, 18, p.113: EN 33
Diglis Lock, 76
Farley, Lavender and Owen,14
Freedom of the City, 101-102, **102**, p.120: EN 26
Gascoine's Seed Merchants, 18
Guildhall, 74, 102
King's School, The, 13
Pearmain (apple), 18
Royal Grammar School, 13, p.113: ENs 35 and 37
Royal Porcelain Company, 32, 50-51, 102, p.120: EN 26
Scientific and Literary Institute, 10
Severn Street, 18
  School of Design, 14
Silver Street Academy, 14, p.113: EN 38
Society of Arts, 11, 16, 18, 30-31
St Andrew's Spire ('Glover's Needle'), 18
St Helen's Parish, 10
St John's Parish, 12, 76, 87
St Peter's Parish, 13
Stella's Brewers, 18
Town Council, 13
Union Club, 67, p.117: EN 4
Vinegar Works, 30
Wordsworth, William (1770-1850), 41, 45
Wye Valley
  Chepstow Castle, 44
  Tintern Abbey, 44-45, **45**

Yates, John E., 84